Praise for *From the Heart of an Abandoned Daughter*

No scholarly book has yet been published that documents the health problems, unhealthy relationship patterns, or self-loathing that children who grow up exposed to a batterer often carry with them through their adult lives. Enter Helen Gennari's groundbreaking memoir. We get to follow that little girl into her adult life. Her voice is so clear and resonant, and her decision to take her private life out into the public view is a gift to all of us.

—Lundy Bancroft
Consultant on domestic abuse and child mistreatment
Author of *When Dad Hurts Mom: Helping Your Children Heal the Wounds of Witnessing Abuse*

This book provides an honest and heartfelt personal account regarding the recovery journey away from childhood powerlessness, due to witnessing domestic violence and maternal emotional neglect, toward a state of power and personal choice in adulthood. Lessons learned include how each of us possesses the ability to make our own choices, and effect our destinies, no matter what has come before.

—Kim Anderson, Ph.D., LCSW
Associate Professor, School of Social Work University of Missouri
Author of *Enhancing Resilience in Survivors of Family Violence*

This is a wonderful guide for empathy and insight toward healing abandonment.

—Susan Anderson
Author of *Black Swan: The Twelve Lessons of Abandonment Recovery*

The journey of healing is a personal one, but it need not be travelled alone. In Helen Gennari's *From the Heart of an Abandoned Daughter*, her vivid and moving stories of a childhood silenced by her father's violence against her mother, lead to an adult's path of healing that others may follow. Like the "mothering tree" that gave her comfort in a comfortless childhood, Helen provides a safe, sturdy and living process for others to use to recover their true selves, their inherent resilience, and their own individual healing.

—Colleen Coble
Chief Executive Officer, Missouri Coalition
Against Domestic and Sexual Violence

This book is a wonderful gift of hope, healing, wisdom and peace for anyone who has grown up with, or is experiencing family violence. The impact of this trauma on innocent children can result in a lifetime lived in fear, isolation, shame and insecurity. Helen invites us, her readers, to accompany her as she shares not only her story but the transformational journey beyond a painful past. Comforted, informed and uplifted, we are empowered to release the bonds of the past in order to embrace a fulfilling, safe, joyful present and future. We deserve nothing less.

—Mary E. Burns
Family violence survivor
Former Executive Director of Woman's Place,
Drop-in Center for abused women, St. Louis, MO

From the Heart of an Abandoned Daughter

My Personal Journey
Through Family Violence
and Beyond

HELEN COLEMAN GENNARI, MSW, LCSW

A Stonebrook Publishing Book

Copyright © Helen Coleman Gennari, 2015

Edited by Nancy L. Erickson
www.TheBookProfessor.com

Cover and interior design by JETLAUNCH
Photograph of author by Suzanne Renner
Illustration of The Rose by Tara Pierce

Library of Congress Control Number: 2014960167
ISBN: 978-0-9830800-4-6
eBook ISBN: 978-0-9830800-5-3

www.HeartOfAnAbandonedDaughter.com

CONTENTS

Part III: The Inner Journey Of the Emotionally Abandoned Child

Part IV: Embracing the Abandoned Self

Part V: Creating a New Life Narrative

AUTHOR'S NOTE

The seven years that it has taken me to dislodge my story from my heart to share it have been a painful but healing journey of returning to myself and knowing for the first time who I really am. Though there is much that I have omitted here, I trust that this glimpse into my childhood and my journey to recovery will be enough to bring hope and healing to my readers. From my heart to yours, I wish you the discovery of your own true and wonderful self.

Helen C. Gennari
April 6, 2015

FOREWORD

S everal years ago a public service announcement ran on late night television that was unlike anything anyone had seen before. All we saw on camera was an adorable little boy, maybe three years old, sitting at the top of the stairs. The rest was all sound.

A man comes home late for dinner—we can hear him come through the door—and he begins to complain that his wife is serving him pizza for dinner. She says if he had called to warn her that he was going to be an hour late, she could have had something else for him, but the meal she originally made was cold now. He's furious about eating pizza, and he begins to throw things around. Well, that's what seems to be happening because, again, we don't see it. But we hear objects smashing, and we hear him yelling, and we hear the woman's desperate voice in her effort to settle him down. And what we do see is powerful; the boy reels with each crashing sound, with each time he hears what sounds like his father hitting his mother, with each time his mother screams. At the end of the ad we hear the mother crying and the father ordering her to clean up the mess that he made. And we see the darkened face of this trembling and confused and—above all, alone—boy on the stairs.

What kind of childhood is this boy going to have? What kind of man will he grow up to be? From what inner turmoil will he suffer as an adult by starting so early in life to carry this fear and pain within him? What does it do to children when they see the person they most love in the world physically wounded and emotionally tortured by their father?

Boys and girls actually have a lot to say on the subject. A British researcher named Caroline McGee interviewed some fifty children and teenagers about their experiences with domestic violence, giving them voice in her book, *Childhood Experiences of Domestic Violence*. We learn how frightened kids feel during the man's assaults. We learn of their love and bitterness; for they love Mom desperately, but they also resent her for not being able to make the violence stop, and for not being able to attend to the children in the midst of her own trauma and panic. In most cases, they feel love and bitterness toward the abuser as well because usually he is their father; they love him and wish he could be a regular dad, and his periodic cruelty causes them to feel a depth of hatred toward him that sometimes reaches murderous proportions.

But what follows after? We actually know very little about how kids go about resolving these internal cross-currents as the years go by, nor have we learned what kinds of pain and dysfunction they carry into their adult lives. (Though we do know that boys who witness battering often grow up to become terrorizers of women themselves, as much as they hated what Dad was doing at the time.) There is no established network of, say, "Adult Children of Battered Women," no therapists who specialize in counseling adults whose father battered their mother. No scholarly book has yet been published that documents the health problems, unhealthy relationship patterns, or self-loathing that children who grow up exposed to a batterer often carry with them through their adult lives.

Enter Helen Gennari's groundbreaking memoir, *From the Heart of an Abandoned Daughter*. Gennari's story brings us into the mental and emotional world of a young girl. We see not just the fear and distress of the child, but also her strengths, her resourcefulness, her ways of keeping her soul alive. Gennari takes us into the inspiring and nourishing relationship that the young girl develops with the natural world, seeking what her caretakers are unable to give her. We see her struggle with trying to understand why her mother seems so unaware of her daughter's needs and her anguish, leaving the girl in a world that feels almost motherless. And we see her exposed, day in and day out, to a father who doesn't care what kind of harm he brings to other people in the family, who demeans Gennari's mother and blames his actions on her, and who takes no heed of his responsibilities as a husband and father.

And then, unique to Gennari's account, we get to follow that little girl into her adult life, through her career, and on into her 70s when it came time to put her life's experiences down in writing. And all of the phases of her life are touched and shaped by the abuse she grew up witnessing.

I am especially moved by the story of Gennari's adult relationship with her mother and the eventual unveiling of decades of silence about the abuse that she and her mother were both devastated by, as victim and as witness. The focus of my professional life for the past ten years has been on trying to publicly expose the least-understood aspect of domestic violence: the range of ways in which abusive men drive mothers and children away from each other. In that context, I have heard dozens of heart-wrenching stories regarding the damage done to relationships. And though it has been less common, I also learn from time to time about the healing of those relationships; inspiring examples of mothers finding their way back to closeness with their sons and daughters. Sometimes the abuser's divisive tricks get revealed. Sometimes the abuser just goes away, allowing a space for healing to take place. And sometimes moms and kids find the language to have the necessary conversations with each other, to speak what could never be spoken before. Through that sharing, they come to understand each other's pain, to understand the many binds that left them not knowing what to do or say, to express the love that was blocked and hidden for so long.

But I've never before had the chance to answer this question: If the healing between mother and child doesn't get a chance to happen while the kids are still at home—is it too late? Can the divide still be crossed years, or even decades later? You'll have to decide what your own answer is as Helen Gennari's story unfolds in the pages ahead.

I hope that Gennari's personal and courageous sharing will contribute to the demand, currently spreading in the modern world, that abusive men be stopped after centuries of societal collusion with their bullying and domination. Her voice is clear and resonant, telling us so much about that boy I described at the top of the stairs, about the girl huddling frightened in her room while her parents scream and dishes are smashed, about the mother who is left so wounded and afraid that she feels that she no longer inhabits the same world as her children. Gennari's decision to take her private life into the public view is a gift to us all.

Lundy Bancroft
Author, workshop leader, and
consultant on domestic abuse and child maltreatment
October, 2014

--------∞∞∞--------

The five books authored by Lundy Bancroft include the following:

Why Does He Do That? Inside the Minds of Angry and Controlling Men

When Dad Hurts Mom: Helping Your Children Heal the Wounds of Witnessing Abuse

PROLOGUE

We shall not cease from exploration
and the end of all our exploring
will be to arrive where we started
and know the place for the first time.

—T.S. Eliot

I recall the desolation I felt when I was at the brink of my forties, with no idea of who I was or where I was headed. I knew there was something very wrong with me—or so I thought. I grew up with this belief, along with the fear that whoever I was would be discovered.

Within each of us is a place where we hold the remains of painful childhood experiences. We lock them away from our awareness and thus, lose touch with our true selves. I only learned this much later in my journey.

I wandered through years of darkness, lost and in search of something. And then one day, many years later, I returned to myself and was forced to acknowledge the pains of my childhood that held me hostage. With help, I breached the wall I had created to shield me from my pain. What I had once thought would devour me, eventually transformed me. I experienced the revelation of a truth that changed me forever. I also learned that I had to look back at where I had come from, if I was to know who I had become.

My experience of growing up in a violent home is a story of transformation and hope. You may relate with the child you meet here. When my story begins, I am in that vulnerable place of early childhood when we are conditioned by the adult messages that both teach us our values and tell us who we are.

I was between the ages of five and six when the abuse started.

I was one of many children who lived in constant terror of an abusive father and was emotionally abandoned by a mother who was preoccupied with survival. My effort to become invisible and survive the situation left me with a distorted sense of self, an image from which I've had to free myself to discover the truth of who I really am.

In Part I, I tell you what happened in our home and how it felt to me as a small child. My memories go back to ages three and four, but my strongest memories are of ages five and six because of my abject loneliness and the fear that accompanied my every breath. It was a time of intense focus that required me to find my own way.

Part II is a compilation of true short stories. Stories are an effective way to pass on values and wisdom since we can wrap them in images that open us to receive the deeper message. These are true stories that embody my childhood experience. I wrote them at various times during my earlier years.

In Part III, I share my inner experience of emotional abandonment, how I learned to abandon myself, and how I eventually learned to stop the process.

Part IV reflects my shift into adulthood and my struggle to transcend the pain of my early years, so I could forgive and begin to heal.

Part V offers resources for anyone who wants to heal and includes a guide for discussion of issues related to family violence.

Throughout the book, I have used some of the poetry that came to me during the years I struggled to heal.

I invite you to join me in this moment, to experience as best you can the transformation of the central character of my story: the small, frightened little girl whose childhood ended between the ages of five and six. Her (my) life journey has been deeply colored by the loss of my mom's emotional presence and protection from my dad's terrifying behavior that she was unable to give to her children.

I have no intent to demonize either of my parents, but rather to give a voice to those of us who may or may not realize that there is an alternative—we don't have to be driven by the painful effects of family violence. My hope is that this will help you understand the effects of family violence and how to be transformed beyond them. My prayer is that my story will awaken the power within you to make choices that heal.

I write these lines long after coming to terms with the early part of my life, aware that I must remain ever-vigilant of that old fear that re-emerges now and then. I reach deep into the trust I have nurtured within myself and simply say, "It's okay; don't be afraid." And always, I remember from whence I've come, with gratitude for all those who love me and continue to help me heal.

Though I've made my home in St. Louis, Missouri, since 1954, my roots are deep within my ancestral home in Old Mines, Missouri. It was the first French settlement in the state, birthed during the late 17th and early 18th centuries.

This was the land of my father's heritage. In 1836, the original land grants were claimed by thirty-one of the early settlers, approved by the U.S. Government, and deeded to those families. One of the persons on the list of claimants was "Widow Coleman," my ancestor.

This region, part of the Louisiana Purchase, was farmed and mined by the people. The land was rocky and poorly suited for farming, so my father's family raised pigs, cows, and chickens, while many of the men were miners. According to one post-Civil War document, the mineral barite, locally called "tiff," was discovered in Washington County, which includes the three neighboring towns of my childhood experience: Old Mines, Potosi, and De Soto.

I still have a few living relatives and friends in that area, and I periodically drive an hour down Highway 21, back in time to my homeland, and marvel at what has never changed. When I reach De Soto, I know I have another twenty minutes or so before I see the familiar gravel roads that reach out to the highway, creeks I've crossed and conversed with many times, tattered buildings that once stood fresh and saluted those who passed through. One of the newer homes belongs to my first-grade teacher, who I still keep in touch with. Six miles south of Old Mines is the town of Potosi. We seldom went there, but this is where we went when we talked about "going into town."

For as long as I can remember, the economy in this area has always been depressed. In the late 1930s, the price of tiff plummeted, which ended several hundred years of small-scale mining. It was the end of an era. The working heritage of my father, his father, and those who came before them was over. When some of the mines closed in 1954, my father found work in St. Louis and moved us there, just as I was ready to start eighth grade.

I struggled to adjust to this relocation. Until then, we lived in a culturally isolated area where French Creole traditions were embraced, and the language of Creole was still spoken by many of the inhabitants, including my paternal grandmother. We were very poor and unaccustomed to the ways of city life.

St. Joachim's Church had been the center of our community life, where the adults gathered outside the entrance after Mass to talk and catch up with the local gossip. Most lived quite a distance away, and only a few people had telephones. The original church, a log building built in 1820, is now the oldest standing church in Missouri. This is where I return to bid a last farewell to folks connected to my family, either through kinship or friendship.

This is the place that shaped me as a child and still holds my roots.

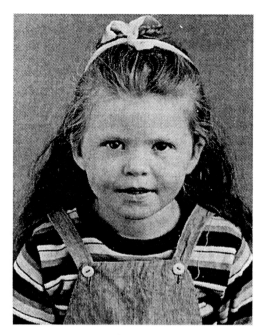

Helen, age 5

It was the trees that saved me. Whenever I could, I ran to the woods where I felt their benevolent welcome to escape my father's violence. I wandered among those tall sentinels the way a baby elephant weaves in and out of the legs of the giant adults, safe and protected. There I felt the connection of the trees and sky and earth and all its creatures. The water, plants, and rocks were my companions, quietly sustaining me in the midst of those terrifying years. The energy of nature's embrace kept calling me back and challenged me to find my way without fearing the bend in the path just up ahead. The silent comfort and interconnectedness of nature made me think that maybe God was really there. I could sit, lean against an old oak, and not say a word. It was a safe and sacred space.

PART I

DISLODGING THE STORY FROM MY HEART

Chapter One

A STORY ROOTED
DEEP IN MY HEART

Journal entry April 8, 2014:

It's been a long, hard winter, with merciless snows and storms that have made me long for spring to assert herself. Outside my window the red bud will soon express her purpleness and off in the distance, a neighbor's yard is fenced with bright yellow forsythia. The house finch is singing her morning song. I feel a surge of hope as I begin this day with gratitude for the seasons that bring us change. So many seasons have passed through my life, leaving me weathered but wiser. I appreciate who I am and my life today with an acceptance that is not "resigned" but "embraces" all that has been, is, and will be.

It's been a long, hard journey, these past seventy-plus years, and I have never felt as peaceful as I do now. At this time of year, my mind returns to the first spring I can remember when, as a small child, I looked up, breathless, into the blossomed peach tree that stood near the old house where we lived. When I closed my eyes, pink was the only color I saw that day. When I close my eyes now, even after all these years, I see and experience my child-self beneath that tree.

I see her stretch her six-year-old body to reach the lowest limb of the tree and pull down a small branch to peer into a clump of peach blossoms. Her eyes brighten as she touches her nose to each deep pink petal. An aura of sadness clings to this child who continues to reach for branches, some unattainable. Finally, she picks one tender blossom, holds it in her hand, and stares at it for a long time. Perhaps she wonders how it grew on the tree or where all that pink came from.

This little one seems lost. She wanders about the place as if she's searching for something. Her head bent low, she looks from side to side, so as not to miss anything. Perhaps she is watching for something or someone. Her movements are slow, deliberate, and she stops now and then to pick up bits of rock or nuts, which she puts into her pocket.

She wanders alone for hours, through the weeds, down by the creek, and into the woods, as if led by some unseen guide who has laid out a journey for her. She seldom smiles, seems content and unafraid, but she is cautious, especially when she lifts a stone or climbs up to sit on a fallen log.

Who is this child who wanders alone? What is she looking for? What goes on in her thoughts, her imagination, her heart? Is she lost? Where does she belong? Does anyone know she is here? Or do they, as I did for years, ignore her?

I have spent the past seventy-plus years getting to know this child, who I now not only claim, but embrace. For years I didn't like her. I was ashamed of her. I refused to accept her. I felt her frailty and disdained her inability to express herself.

The shame I felt from all that had transpired during those early years has been something I have tried to hide, even from myself. And yet, what I have so resolutely denied has, in the end, defined me. Until now.

Though seven decades have passed—seasons of sultry summers and weary winters—I close my eyes and hear evening sounds so similar to those recorded deep within my aging bones. I invite you to join me as I return to the days when I was this small child who wondered about everything I saw and heard, from the ground up.

Like an old family movie abandoned to some cluttered corner of the attic, some would say the details of my journey should be left undisturbed to disintegrate to dust. I would actually prefer that. But too many children have been emotionally abandoned, cared for by a mom who simply struggled to survive. Too many little hearts have been broken. Too many little ones have been there, terrified by the sights and sounds of their mom being hurt by the man they called "Dad." Too many of these children have been broken by the trauma of family violence and have grown up wounded by its ongoing effects. I offer my story to acknowledge them, and to give them hope that they can be transformed from their life of pain.

I, too, once stood with no voice, unable to speak or scream for help. My heart ached with sadness. I was afraid and confused when no one noticed my tears and isolation. Through a torturous journey that began at age sixteen when I left home, I have finally found my voice and can no longer remain silent. My story is that of so many children, then and now. We were emotionally abandoned by our mothers, our only lifeline, often without her even being aware of it because she used every ounce of her energy to simply survive the abuse. Her husband's abuse betrayed their commitment. She was abandoned by him and had to fend for herself. To save herself and her children, she had to emotionally abandon herself and her children and make choices she hoped would please her batterer, thinking she could minimize the abuse. In turn, the abandoned child had to abandon herself in order to survive. She had to hide her true self, her true feelings, and pretend to be okay in an effort to feel safe. She would grow into an adult, imprisoned by fear, aware only of the shadow of who she really was.

Had I been a boy, my experience might have been different, due to the dictates of society. I might have learned that this was how women were to be treated, that they were to be abused. Or, I may have been inclined to exercise my bravado and intervene when Mom was being beaten. As it was, I learned early to be silent, to tell no one what I saw and heard those terrifying nights when I covered my ears to close out the sounds of my mother's pain, wondering if she would still be alive when it was over.

At the age of six, I made my first major decision. I stood at the top of the stairs and listened to my dad attack my mom, and I had to decide whether or not to go down and help her.

I chose not to go down because I was afraid my father would also hurt, or even kill, me. I carried the guilt of this decision well into my adult life.

As the oldest of three, I felt responsible for my two little sisters and wanted to protect them. I often tried to distract them from the terror we could not escape. Our very old house had no insulation to absorb the sounds of the beatings and our mother's cries, so I told them stories. And when I had exhausted the stories I'd been told and had memorized, I made up new stories, always with happy endings.

This—my story—is not made up. Those years of terror had long been buried, but they are rooted in the depths of my heart, to be recalled as I reflected on and tried to make sense of my early family experiences. In the meantime, my parents have passed on to what is hopefully a place of peace. My sisters and I are each on our own journey to heal, a process that is ongoing and different for each of us. I have come to appreciate not only the journey, but also the lessons learned as I at first resisted, then persisted, and eventually allowed myself to trust and connect with others in my life. The only happy endings are those we choose to create. I have written a new script for my life, reflected in this book, so that you see not only my pain, but most of all, the transformation that has changed my life and is possible for you, too.

Chapter Two

LIFE BEFORE THE INVASION

Some of my earliest childhood memories are of the time we spent on my maternal grandmother's farm while she was temporarily living elsewhere. I was only three or four years old, but I have vivid memories of this time. Mom was always close by. Sometimes I would crawl up on her lap and feel her arms around me. She wore a necklace made of brown plastic leaves that I liked to play with while she held me. On Sunday mornings, I would stand near her and watch her put on her makeup. My head barely reached the base of her vanity as I watched her put on lipstick and blot it with a tissue. On cold winter evenings, I knelt on a chair next to the kitchen table and wondered as I watched mom draw. She drew lines with a pencil that eventually revealed a house and a picket fence adorned with a climbing rose bush. Perhaps it was the place she dreamed would be ours when my dad returned from overseas.

Mom, my sister Carol, and I lived at Grandma's house while my dad was in some far away country "fighting in a war," as Mom said, and I wondered what a "war" was. The old farmhouse had once belonged to the local doctor, so it was large with many rooms. Mom's brother, Uncle Jimmy, lived with his wife and six children in the largest part of the house. Grandma's section consisted of two rooms. The kitchen connected her living space to the main house, like a small afterthought. A second room served as a living room/bedroom combo. On the east side there was a porch that ran the length of her section of the building. The floor was made of concrete, only a few inches off the ground. We played there when it rained or when it was too hot for us to be in the sun. The nearby cellar door and a rain barrel were part of the fun.

There was a door on the west side that opened from the kitchen to the back of the house, where there was a path that led to the vegetable garden a few yards away. The kitchen window had no curtains and was always open, welcoming the fragrance of the white blossoms on the large mock orange bush just outside the door. A large patch of basil grew nearby. Every Saturday morning these fragrances competed with the aroma of freshly baked bread and cinnamon rolls that cooled on the round, wooden table near the window.

I loved the vegetable garden. When spring came, and it was the right time, the ground was ploughed and readied for the plants. We all gathered for the planting; the tomatoes were my favorites. Uncle Jimmy and Aunt Mary put a stick at the end of each long row, then tied a string from one stick to the other as a guide to keep the rows straight. Mom dug small holes in the soil several inches apart and poured in water. We little ones were shown how to drop the plants in the holes, then dip our hands into the mud and pat it to form a solid base around the new plant.

For months, we weeded and watered and watched the plants grow. When the vines were heavy with ripeness, we gathered the red fruit into bushel baskets for our mothers to can for the winter months. Of course, many of the tomatoes fell from the over-laden baskets. Right there in the garden, we bit into their lush, ripe skin and ate them like candy.

We were one big family, sharing space, meals, and chores. When our tasks were done, we ran barefoot through the fields, played hide-and-seek in the hayloft and under the ancient lilac bushes. I loved to play in the creek and catch tadpoles. Summer days were long and hot but never long enough. We explored the woods and the fields, swam in the creek, and picked wildflowers. We did have to show up for meals. My six cousins were great playmates. The oldest girl was three months older than me and to this day, is like a sister. These were my pre-school days, ages three to four, and they were full of carefree, childhood play.

My sister, Carol, was a year younger than me. Mom gave us a lot of attention when she wasn't in the kitchen or out in the fields. She made our clothes from flower-patterned flour sacks, and then created hair bows that matched our dresses. She took pictures of us with her Brownie camera and sent them off to Dad. We played guessing games with her, and I often begged her, "Mom, tell us about when you were a little girl," to which she would reply, "Well, a long, long time ago..." "Were you really little like us, Mom?" I just couldn't imagine her as a child.

Sometimes we listened to her play her guitar and sing. She had a beautiful clear, strong voice. When I wasn't at play with my cousins, I was wherever Mom was. I watched her sew or played on the floor with my toys, while she ironed and listened to the soaps on the radio. This short period in my life was a time when I felt like I "belonged." I felt safe and carefree as I played with my little sister and cousins. It was an idyllic time of stability and closeness to Mom.

But I missed my father and recall that I slept with his picture under my pillow. I would talk about him to anyone who would listen. "My daddy is in the war." I had no idea what that meant, since I had no concept of "war" and no sense of how far away he was. I could tell that mom missed him, too. She wrote many letters and seemed happy when he wrote back. I think my little sister was too young to understand any of this.

The day he left, dressed in his Army uniform, he presented me with a little toilet seat he had made for me out of a wooden orange crate. He knew I was afraid to sit in the outhouse. It was also hard for me to climb up on the seat that was made for adults. I remember how confused I was because I felt glad for the little seat but sad that he was leaving. We stood and watched him walk away—up the hill to the road where someone picked him up and took him to the train station in town. World War II had reached into our life.

I can't remember how long he was gone. It seemed like forever, and I sometimes wondered if he would ever come home. And then, one day, I caught sight of him. He was coming across the field, walking from the road where someone had dropped him a few miles away. I remember the excitement and the tears. One at a time, he held my sister and me on his lap, giving us little gifts he had brought with him. Mom stood by and watched with such a look of happiness on her face. That scene is engraved in my heart as a special moment of warmth and joy for us as a family.

It was never repeated.

I was four years old and had no idea what my father experienced during the war. He never talked about it except to tell us that he had always carried our picture with him, even past the "white cliffs of Dover." It was years before I understood what he was talking about. He had pictures of his buddies in uniform, taken in some far away country; pictures of natives in those countries; pictures we were not meant to see that I discovered later in an old trunk one rainy day when I explored his mother's attic.

Shortly after my father returned, he took us from this place and moved us in with his mom and dad. The general rule in our family was "children are to be seen but not heard." No one ever told us the when, where, or why of anything, including where we were going or why. I just recall being relocated one day and thinking this log cabin was our new home. There were three rooms for the six of us, with no indoor plumbing or electricity. Grandma lit the coal oil lamp each evening when darkness began to fall. She used the oil sparingly, always aware of its cost. Mom and

Dad slept in an old bed in a tiny room used for storage. My sister and I slept on an old sofa in the kitchen. Grandma and Grandpa occupied the only bedroom in the house. During the day, we had space to play in the woods and fields, but it was much less than before. I missed my cousins terribly but even more, I missed Mom, who was no longer available to be with us.

Mom had gotten a job at the factory in town while my father took a job at the nearby tiff mill where his dad worked. Grandma became our caregiver. She was not the best cook or housekeeper, but she was great as a grandma. On those hot, summer days before I started first grade, she gave us strawberry Kool-Aid made with the fresh water I carried from the spring at the bottom of the hill. One of my chores was to periodically go to the spring for a bucket of the cold water, which I then placed on a table on her porch. Above it hung a large dipper that everyone drank from when they were thirsty.

Except for the occasional argument between my grandmother and her alcoholic husband, our daily life was fairly comfortable in this new setting. However, I did miss my cousins and our play together. In this new place, I rarely included my little sister in my outdoor play. Instead, I wandered alone in the woods and fields where I explored. I found bird nests, berry patches, and ponds, picked wild daisies, and followed animal tracks along the muddy edge of the creek.

The little creek ran through the property on the edge of the nearby woods, and it was my favorite companion on those hot summer days without playmates. For hours, I experimented with ways to arrange the rocks and mud to dam up the water and create pools of clear crystal liquid. "Where did you come from?" I would ask the creek, and "Where will you go?" If I waited too long to release the water, it simply flowed over and beyond my little dam, determined to continue its journey to some mysterious destination. In those moments, as I watched and wondered, time stood still. I was lost in the water and the stones over which it flowed. I longed to follow the little stream and find out where it went or to find out where it came from.

One day, I walked along its bank to find the place where it started to flow. Was it a hole in the hillside, or did it come up out of a pile of rocks? Did it look the same there as it did here? I walked on. When the sun began to sink behind the trees, darkness fell on this unfamiliar place where I had wandered. I knew I needed to go back home while I could still see. My heart still holds the desire to find the beginning of that little creek. I often wonder if it is still there, waiting to be discovered.

I not only connected with nature, but also with my paternal grandma, the only adult who on occasion had time for me. She seldom laughed, often appeared deep in thought, and prayed a lot. Sometimes we walked the four or five miles to church together for Mass and devotions. The parish church was located in the French mining town of Old Mines, just outside the small town of Potosi, Missouri.

We walked along Highway 21, usually in silence. Occasionally a car or truck would stop, and a complete stranger would offer us a ride, which we gladly accepted. It always felt special to have this time with my grandma.

Some nights, we sat on the porch for long hours to avoid using too much lamp oil. I loved these moments when she held me on her lap and told me stories about the stars overhead, stories passed down, no doubt, from an ancestor who was a Cherokee Indian.

One night, when grandma finished her stories, she told me that I would start to school soon. "You will go to Cruise School where I studied many years ago. You will learn to read books and write your name."

I thought for a while and then asked, "What's it like, Grandma, and where is it?"

"The school is a white, two-room building on Highway 21, a few miles from here. You know the Johnsons who live up on the hill?" I shook my head yes. "Well, Rose Ann will be your teacher." That September I was five years old and would turn six in November.

On the first day of school, I was filled with both anxiety and excitement as I sat with about twenty other children in a room with few windows and the smell of chalk. We were grades one to four. Grades five to eight were in the second room.

After morning recess, we all returned to our assigned seats. Then, Miss Johnson called all the first graders to the front of the room. She motioned for us to gather around her desk. There were nine girls and boys, all with eager faces and no idea of what was about to happen. "I have a surprise for you today," she said, as she smiled and handed a book to each of us. I looked at my first book in awe. I held it with both my hands. It smelled new, like tree bark, picked just after an early morning rain. It had a picture of a little girl, a little boy, and a dog called "Spot."

"Children, would you like to learn to read today?" our teacher asked enthusiastically. She seemed so young. I learned years later that she was just out of high school, and we were her first class. We shook our heads eagerly and answered in sing-song unison, "Yes, Miss Johnson."

She opened her book and directed us to do the same. And then she began to read to us. She had us repeat the words and sentences after her. This ritual occurred every afternoon of our first month of school. And then we were given the opportunity to pick out a storybook from the library that was in the front right corner of our classroom behind the old wood stove. I chose one that had a little red-haired girl on the cover, sitting in a strawberry patch. I couldn't wait to see if I could read it.

I soon discovered that storybooks were like open doors, and I could go places I had never been and meet people I could otherwise never meet. Books would eventually become one of my favorite escapes from the violence that eventually invaded our family.

That first school year passed quickly, and I loved the adventure of learning. The summer months that followed seemed to drag. I couldn't wait to go back to school in September.

One night, at the end of September, 1947, Mom was rushed to the hospital while my sister and I slept. She was gone for almost a week, and I missed our time together when she would sit and listen to me read. She finally returned home, with a little bundle in her arms. A new baby sister! Mom said her name was Janice Faye. I begged to hold her and eventually was allowed to. Janice was like a real, live doll, and all I wanted to do was hold her and play with her. In time, Mom taught me how to change her diaper and feed her, too.

My 1947–1948 school term flew by. Janice had just turned one year old when my father decided it was time to move to our own place. Mom packed up our few belongings, put them and us into the old Model T car, and our dad drove us to the place we still call "the old house on the hill."

As we rode across several large fields away from our grandparents' home, I did not know that this journey marked the end of my childhood. The carefree life I had known was soon to be displaced by persistent fear and complete isolation in a place where there was seldom a visitor. We were about to experience an invasion we could not escape.

Chapter Three

THE INVASION

ejected and forlorn, the old house sat on the crest of a hill that sloped off into fields of endless wild grass. What we saw when we arrived was a shell of a house that was weather-beaten, surrounded by weeds, and had been neglected for years. It would take weeks to gather the trash left by hunters, pull the weeds, and make necessary repairs in the house. No one had lived there for years. The gray wood siding had become un-nailed in places. The windows were clouded with accumulated dust and spider webs. I wondered how old it was, who had lived there, and why they had abandoned what had once been a stately building.

The old house was about a mile and a half away from anyone. Another family lived several miles north, and there was a family about a mile to the south. It seemed so far away from everything. No matter where I looked, all I could see was wild grass, bushes, trees, and sky. A nearby barn had a rusted roof that slanted down close to the ground. The house itself looked haunted.

Despite its desolate deterioration, we moved in, and this became our new home. Dad unloaded the boxes with clothes, pots and pans, dishes, and food. "Mom, where will we put our stuff?" I asked, as we walked through the empty rooms. There were no cabinets or furniture.

"Grandma is going to give us a cabinet she's not using," she said. "As soon as we have the money, we will get some furniture. It will all work out."

In the meantime, my dad found two old saw horses in the barn. He laid several battered wooden planks across them to form our table. It was a long time before we had a real table and chairs or other needed furniture.

For the first couple of months, we worked hard to clean up the property, make the old house livable, and eventually established a routine that would be our new life. I missed time with my grandma and her stories. I missed the little creek.

There were two upstairs rooms that were reached by rickety steps my father eventually replaced. One room was used for storage. Its walls were so thin we could actually look through cracks and see the yard outside. The second room was in better condition, and it became the bedroom shared by my two sisters and me.

The two downstairs rooms became the kitchen and our parents' bedroom. The worn sofa that we had slept on in Grandma's kitchen was put in their room, which then doubled as our living room. The old potbelly stove in the corner of their room blocked the outside door during the winter months. On cold winter evenings, this provided a small, private corner where we bathed in a tin tub that Mom filled from a kettle she heated on the stove. We moved the stove out when summer arrived.

We had no electricity, so in the nearby forest my father chopped wood that we used to keep us warm and cook our meals. We didn't have a source of water, so we drove through the fields, back to our grandparents' spring, and filled large, metal milk cans with the water we needed to drink, cook, and bathe. On occasion, my sister Carol and I walked through the fields and carried the water home in tin buckets. My father eventually had the old well on the property cleaned so that we had our own source.

Shortly after we moved in, we added a white cow with brown spots to the family. Josie provided our milk, and it was my job to churn the milk into butter. I sat on the floor with the glass churn between my legs and turned the handle, fascinated as I watched the white, foamy liquid thicken and change into a solid ball of butter.

One night, our dad brought home three chickens and a rooster he had won in a card game, and our sources of food were further increased.

We planted a garden in the large open field down the hill in front of the house. The work never ended as we fell into a routine of planting, feeding, weeding, gathering, and carrying wood and water.

I never saw my mom sit down with a cup of coffee. When she wasn't at her factory job in town doing assembly line piecework, she spent herself for us. She cooked, cleaned, canned, washed, ironed, and at the end of the day went out to find the cow and then milked her.

The local tiff mill had provided work for several generations of my dad's family. His job was to drive a large machine that dug up the soil and deposited it into the dump trucks that took it to the mill where it was processed to remove the tiff (barite). It was dirty, dangerous work for which he was paid very little.

One night, I overheard my mom and dad arguing. Mom's words were too soft to understand, but I heard the word "money." My dad had been drinking and spoke loudly. "Stop bitching. I've worked hard all day and don't want to hear it. I gave you money last week for groceries."

"And I told you it wasn't enough. We're getting behind with other bills that need to be paid. We'd have enough if you didn't drink it all up."

"It's none of your damn business if I decide to stop after work and have a drink with the guys."

"All I'm saying is—"

"I've had it with you, damn it."

The next sound I heard was a series of slaps and my mother's voice muffled. It sounded like they were struggling, and she was trying to get away from him. And then silence. My heart pounded loudly, and I felt sick to my stomach as I chose not to go inside. I was glad my little sisters were down by the garden. I sat for a while out in the yard, stunned by what had just happened. Eventually, I joined my sisters, but it was getting dark, and we would have to go in soon. From that time on, I worried about my mom—and money—and felt really helpless.

Some months before this, my dad started to come home late from work. He was more sullen than usual, was withdrawn, and he never smiled. He argued more with Mom. He scolded us for the slightest noise we made while doing the supper dishes. If Mom didn't respond immediately when he called her, or if she said anything resistant to his demand for her to do something, he would fly into a rage. This might begin with a verbal attack, followed by striking her across the face. His physical size and sporadic anger were his weapons of intimidation. We began to live in constant fear of triggering his attacks.

It was a summer of major transition, and as I prepared to go back to school, I was filled with anxiety about my father's behavior and about what my new school would be like. Mom had decided, after a visit from the Pastor of St. Joachim's parish, to send Carol and me to the Catholic school. My first day of second grade dawned with clouds of fear.

After what felt like a long bus ride up Highway 21, we were directed to a small building near the church that housed the first two grades. The remaining six grades were crowded into a white frame building near the site where a new school was being built.

Carol sat with the first graders on one side of the one-room schoolhouse; I sat with the second graders on the other side of the room. Sister Henrietta's gruff manner and threats to punish us if we didn't keep quiet were all too familiar to the two of us.

Each morning after Dad left to go to work, Mom walked through the woods to the highway to catch a ride to town where she worked at the doll factory. It was my responsibility to get myself and Carol ready for school, close up the house, and take our little Janice, almost two, to Grandma's, where she would spend the day. Carol and I dropped her off on the way to our bus stop, and then walked another mile to Highway 21 to wait for the school bus.

At the end of the day, I looked forward to walking home from the bus stop. It took about forty minutes to get home, and I liked to linger at Grandma's little creek that meandered through the field we crossed. Sometimes the creek was full of yesterday's rain and the green, mossy banks called to me. I sat and dangled my tired feet in the slow flow of the stream and watched the tadpoles flit in and out of the dead leaves that were caught in roots along the bank. They tickled my toes, as if daring me to catch them. I once caught a few of the slimy little creatures and put them in a coffee jar. When their tails began to disappear, Mom said, "Helen, if you don't let them go, they will hop out on their own." I thought about how I would miss them. I thought about how I missed my cousins, and how much I missed Mom when she was gone to work. She was always so tired when she got home.

When the sun started to disappear behind the trees, I knew we needed to get home. My worry about Mom and the danger I felt at home was like a heavy hand that reached for me through-out the day. Now, it gripped me, and my stomach tightened as I climbed the hill to the old gray house, Carol at my side.

Mom always picked up Janice on the way home from work and was usually the first one home. When we walked into the kitchen, it was hot and full of the aromas of fried potatoes and stewed tomatoes. Mom opened the oven of the wood-burning stove to check the biscuits as she wiped her flushed face. She turned and threw me that "where-have-you-been" look. The table should have been set by now. I dropped my school bag on a chair and hurriedly opened the cabinet door. I moved quickly to prepare the table while the memory of the cool stream faded under my guilt for being late to help Mom.

She and I usually worked in silence, and I wondered if her thoughts were like mine. *He's not home yet. I'm glad. I like it when we have Mom to ourselves. I like it when he isn't here, hollering at her or making us rub his feet. Maybe he won't come home tonight. Maybe he'll stay at the tavern or wherever he is. Maybe we can sit outside after supper, and Mom will tell us stories about when she was a little girl. She smiles when he's not here. Please, God, don't let him come home tonight.*

We always began our meal in silence, grateful for his absence, but our anxiety was like a black cloud that hung over us. He might arrive at any moment. Even when he wasn't around, his meanness infected our space.

"We might go to my mom's farm this weekend, if it's okay with your dad," Mom said one evening as we finished our meal.

"That means we'll get to see our cousins again!" I announced with excitement. I wondered why we ever left them; we were so happy there. "Mom, do you think he will let us go?"

"I don't know. It depends on what mood he's in this weekend." While we did our after-supper chores, Carol and I talked about what we would do if we got to go to the farm.

One evening as I was about to do my chores, Mom asked me to go with her to get the cow. I felt special, chosen to go with Mom. I followed her silently and wondered why—why did she ask me to go with her? We walked in silence through the tall summer-dry grass for a while before she turned to me with an anxious look. "Remember when you asked me about your dad's sister, Aunt Dorothy?"

"Yes, I remember." We were coming home from church one Sunday. "I asked you why her tummy was so big, and you said that someday you would explain."

"Well, I talked with the priest last Sunday, and he said you are old enough for me to tell you this. Aunt Dorothy is going to have a baby in about a month." That's all Mom said. I still had no idea what that had to do with my aunt's sudden weight gain.

We walked the cow home in silence. I wondered what Mom was thinking. As for me, I had more questions, unable to ask them, not sure she wanted to hear them.

So, is the baby in her tummy? If so, how did it get there? How will it get out? Does it hurt? How long does it take? Are you going to have another baby?

It would be a few more years before I learned what a big tummy had to do with a new baby. I was in seventh grade when the mystery unraveled at school one day. My teacher took the girls to a separate classroom and showed us a movie. It told us all about menstruation, how our bodies would change, and how this prepared us to eventually have babies. I knew I would never have a baby because I would never marry. I would never put myself in my mom's position—never.

Mom finished the milking as the stars began to flicker overhead, like candles in the sky. It was quiet, serene. And then I heard the sound of his car as it climbed the hill. My stomach tightened. Mom ran inside to the kitchen, where she kept his supper hot on the wood stove. Even in the horrid heat of summer, she kept the fire burning low, in order to give him a hot meal whenever he showed up.

From the scowl on his face and his unsteady gait when he walked through the door, I knew that the calm of our evening was over. A dark silence shrouded the room as he sat down at the table. This was my signal to leave. I gathered my sisters and took them outside.

"Oh, please God, let him go to sleep soon. Don't let him argue with Mom. And please, don't let her talk back to him. It always gets worse when she does that."

Ever since we moved to this isolated place, Dad often went to the local tavern after work and then came home late for supper, drunk. In this condition, it was impossible to reason with him. If Mom tried to talk with him about being late for supper, he verbally abused her. They had many arguments related to his drinking, coming home late, and the lack of money. His anger soon morphed into rage. He criticized the food, even though Mom had gone to great lengths to keep it hot. At times, he threw his plate of food across the room. I was terrified of his rage.

If it wasn't too late at night, I would take my little sisters outside and walk until we couldn't hear their arguments. I tried to distract them with some form of play, but it was useless. How could we play when something so awful was going on inside the house? Though we had left the space that felt dangerous, Mom was still in there, and part of me was in there with her. I worried about what would happen to her. And then I had to decide when it was safe for us to go back into the house.

I dreaded the time of day when he was supposed to come home. We never knew what would happen when he walked in. If he was "lovey dovey" with Mom and nice to us, we were greatly relieved. This night might be okay. There were some nights that began this way. But I always waited for when he would get enraged and say bad things to Mom. I knew what would come next.

One such calm evening, Carol and I sat at the table doing our homework, while Janice leaned over her coloring book intently coloring a tree with big red apples. Suddenly, from the other room, "You bitch! You can't do anything right. Give me that."

Next—the sound of glass shattered; he had thrown something through the window. We sat frozen in our chairs. Mom's response was muffled. This triggered a volley of curses, followed by, "God damn you. Who do you think you are?" And then I heard the sound of him striking her, the sound of her falling to the floor. The sound of him grunting as he kicked her terrified me.

"Stop, stop, you're hurting me. Get off of me." Silence. And then, between sobs, she pleaded, "Let me go! Let go of me."

I picked up my little sister Janice as she began to cry, and pulled Carol toward me as tears filled her eyes. It was too dark to go outside. My heart pounded loudly, as if it, too, wanted out. I fought back my own tears that I didn't want my sisters to see, as I took them up the steps to our attic room.

Our room was bleak. It had only a bed that we shared and a wooden orange crate that I had converted into a place to keep some books I found in Grandma's attic. The few clothes we had were kept in boxes, one for each of us. The walls were as bare as the plank floor, and there was one small window with dusty panes that let in far less light than we needed.

After we went up to our room at night, Mom usually came up with the oil lamp, which I would eventually dim to let the flame burn low through the night. Sometimes she couldn't come up, and we would lay together in the dark and try to fall asleep. Those were the nights when we heard the sounds of our dad yelling as he beat Mom. Her cries would seep up through the cracks in our floor. On those nights, we could not sleep. I hugged my little sisters close and tried to block out the sound by telling them a story that would hopefully distract them. They didn't care that they had already heard my stories. They curled up close to me as I told those stories over and over again.

In time, things quieted down, and I could stop telling stories, but I seldom went to sleep. So much to think about, so much to worry about. *I didn't get my homework done tonight. Sister Bridget will scold me tomorrow. I hope Mom is okay. Maybe I should go downstairs and check on her. I am afraid to go down. What if he hurts me, too?*

On other nights, he went directly to bed, and we went upstairs with a sense of relief, only to be awakened during the night by raised voices coming from their room. It often escalated to sounds that terrified me. If my sisters were asleep, I covered my head with a pillow to drown out the sounds. *"Oh God, please, please make him stop."* As always, I thought that I should go down to protect Mom, but fear held me back. I didn't know what to do, and the guilt of not going down haunted me for years.

I don't think I cried much on those nights. I couldn't let my sisters see me cry. Sometimes I lay there and listened to them sleep, watching the moonlight push its way through the little window, despite its dingy darkness. I was drawn to the pool of light the moon created on the floor. Careful not to wake my sisters, I would slowly crawl out of bed and sit on the floor in that little patch of moonlight. It had come all the way from the moon, way far up in the sky, just to land here in my darkness and be with me. I would sit there until the light disappeared, and then I was usually very tired.

Sometime I was so weary that I couldn't sleep. I watched the oil lamp cast ghostly shadows on the wall and wondered about tomorrow. Curled up next to me, Janice would move restlessly. *She will be two years old in October. So little. So innocent. Mom and Dad hardly ever pick her up, so I hold her on my lap a lot. Her blond curls are easy to comb. Her chubby legs are getting stronger every day. I like to play school, and I can't wait till she's old enough for me to teach her the ABCs.*

Even though I was only six, I knew I needed to make things better, but the most I could do was try to protect my little sisters. I spent many nights awake trying to figure things out. *What did I do that caused these awful things to happen? Was there something more I needed to do? Was my mother hurt? What if she is dead? What will happen to us? Will we have to live with him?* I knew I didn't want to. I was so afraid of him. When morning came, I was afraid to go downstairs—afraid of what I would see when I went down to breakfast. One morning, I looked up at the kitchen ceiling and saw four holes where the legs of a chair had punctured the ceiling. *He must have raised the chair to hit Mom.*

Many nights I was terrified of what was going on downstairs and what might happen to all of us. My mother, my lifeline, was being brutally beaten by someone who happened to be my father, someone who lived with us and said he loved us. Morning after morning, I went to the breakfast table unsure of what to expect. I could almost taste the leaden silence, while Mom, her back to us, stirred the fried potatoes. She would serve us breakfast as if nothing had ever happened. I ate, my eyes focused on my plate, confused by the mixture of feelings—anger at my father for hurting Mom and bruising her face, relief and sheer joy that she was still alive.

This was a common scenario during those grade-school years when we lived in the old house on the hill. My mom had been beaten. There might be bruises on her arms, or her lip would be swollen, or she might have a new limp. Despite these visible signs, not a word was ever spoken about it, not even once. And I couldn't ask because I didn't know what to say. I didn't know how to talk about it or express my anger. And I was angry. It was an anger that grew within me, but I buried it deep under the cover of my need to please and to be perfect.

Chapter Four

ABANDONED

S ometimes when I approached our old house, I wondered who had been there before us. Was there a mom and dad and kids? How long were they there? Were they happy, and why did they leave? It had certainly been a long time since anyone lived within those vacated rooms, with their thin walls and no interior doors to shut out the sound. It looked like it had never been painted in some spots. The bare floorboards complained when we walked on them. The three exterior doors had no locks, and we had to step up on an old cinder block to reach them. The foundation was made of rocks that someone had laid in place with nothing to hold them together. Many of the stones did not fit well, and yet this abandoned abode had obviously weathered many seasons before we arrived.

The seasons I remember there were all painful. I measured them by school years, second to seventh grade. Years that might have been filled with the excitement of an ever-expanding world of discovery and playmates and childishness were, instead, a time when we were terrorized and lived in fear. I was always on edge, afraid of what might happen, and when my fears were realized, I was plunged into the depths of the darkest aloneness imaginable. This was especially true when my father made another brutal attack on Mom. I had a fierce need to hide myself and this awful reality from everyone. No one must ever know what took place at my house.

The energy I should have used to play was spent trying to figure out what to do or not do, as if by some magical formula I could make it all better. Because I could tell no one what went on in my home, I had to figure it all out by myself. And I was only six. It was a bleak and lonely place to be, this life in the old house on the hill.

This is not to say that I never played or felt the companionship of other children. I did have the opportunity to play with other children at school, my temporary escape from home, though I was never good at play. I was extremely shy, determined to avoid any close connection with anyone lest I be found out, so my social skills were limited. I watched the other children interact with ease, while I had to force myself just to walk into a group and join them. It was easier to simply go sit in the quiet of the church, which I often did. They never missed me: No one ever looked for me or asked where I had been. I became invisible. And even though there was a part of me that worked to create that illusion, it was a lonely, abandoned place to be, there in that vast space of possibilities with only one thing on my mind: *How will things be when Dad comes home tonight?*

While I loathed the discomfort of a group situation, I excelled in the classroom, as long as I didn't have to perform publicly. I felt like an outcast and needed to be invisible, so I rarely raised my hand for fear I would be called upon. I was sure I would say or do something wrong. This conviction reached deep into my soul, and I believed I was inferior to everyone else.

I dreaded to hear the sound of my name and cringed when my name was spoken. Because I did not want to call attention to myself, there were many questions I had but did not ask. I paid a price for this in the years that followed, when I needed to know the things I had not learned because I didn't ask questions. It took years for me to change that pattern and learn to speak up, which became even more painful as I got older and realized how much my silence isolated me. I had become an island, unreachable by anyone, especially myself.

I was always on the outside looking in, separate and alone, missing out on something—perhaps everything. I knew that something was wrong with me. The self-imposed barrier that I erected separated me from everyone else but gave me the protection I so desperately needed. I could see that I was missing out on the life that went on around me. I felt my social ineptness, which held me back and prevented me from connecting with the others. I also blamed myself each time I failed to join in.

I occupied a space no one else could enter. I had no voice. I was invisible. I was so afraid of everything and everyone, and I began to avoid other people when I could. At age fifteen, I wrote, "I hate people" in my journal.

Being separated from my family and peers was agonizing. I could neither understand the overpowering sense of isolation that clouded my life, nor could I escape it. No matter where I was or what I did, I felt isolated, and I was sure that it was because something was wrong with me. *I'm bad, and no one could ever like me. I don't like me.*

It would be years before I realized how disconnected I was from myself. I was acutely aware of the distance between me and my peers, a distance that was magnified in any group setting, particularly at school. I loved school, but I dreaded being there. I was never, not for one moment, free of the fear of rejection. It was a black cloud that followed me everywhere.

Because of the bus ride home from school followed by my walk home through the fields, I had lots of time to mull over the day's events. I criticized myself for how I had handled some things and puzzled over others. Now and then I was pleased by something I had done at school and was eager to tell Mom all about it, but I knew I wouldn't. Sometimes, I celebrated with a romp through the October leaves strewn across my path. The crunching leaves and the sweet aroma released by these discarded bits of nature were a balm of comfort after a stressful day.

Although Carol walked at my side, I was totally absorbed in my own thoughts and often forgot she was there. I wonder if she felt abandoned by me.

When we got home, Mom would be at the woodstove in the kitchen. She was a good cook, just like her mother. And like her mother, Mom spent a lot of her time in the kitchen, the main room of the house. This was where we did our homework and played cards and other games at the table in the evening. This is where we lived until bedtime, if we weren't outside. My time with Mom was usually in the kitchen. Countless times, I watched her roll out biscuit dough or cut up and arrange chicken to be fried. Sometimes I helped her peel the potatoes we ate at almost every meal.

This was done in a silence that separated us, but at the same time, it leant a sense of intimacy—the kind that exists between two people who are close and don't need to talk. But I needed to talk; maybe Mom did, too. I wanted to tell her about the good grade I got or how John knocked me down on the playground and how my shoulder still hurt. And then there was the first time I slid down a slide. I didn't know I needed to put my feet down to catch myself, so I fell flat on the ground, hit my head on the edge of the slide, and blacked out. A watchful teacher tried to carry me off the playground but eventually put me down at my insistence as I came out of my stunned condition. I wanted Mom to know that I was brave enough to go back and do the slide again, this time using my feet to catch myself. But she never asked about my day at school, and I never told her. It all faded into the darkness of our struggle to survive my father's abuse.

Instead, I thought about what happened the night before and wondered if she was really okay after being beaten so badly. I didn't ask. It wasn't the thing to do. Mom's silence hid so much and yet, communicated a strong message: We don't talk about this.

I guess not talking about it made it easier for her, like it hadn't really happened. But I knew what happened. I had heard my father's loud, demeaning words. I had heard the blows and her effort to muffle her cries. I had seen the bruises she tried to cover. I carried all of this, a heavy burden in my heart, as something that I, too, must hide and never speak of.

So I stood silently beside her all of those grade school evenings and watched her prepare the evening meal. Though I felt the distance between us, I felt ever so protective of her, forgetting the things I wanted to tell her. Of all people, I wanted her to know. But she had too much to deal with, and I didn't want to add to her burden. I never stopped worrying about her. I worried that one day my dad would kill her and we would be left alone with this crazy man.

In today's terms, our dad was a terrorist. His very presence was a continual threat, and we knew the full impact of what he could do. I came to dread his presence, and I prayed that he wouldn't come home at night. But he always did. When he was at home, I was on constant alert for his next eruption. Whether he was yelling, throwing things, or attacking Mom, I had to be ready to make a decision about what to do.

When he was home, we had to be very quiet. We often had to stay outside. Nothing but what *he* wanted mattered, and when things didn't happen as he wanted, someone suffered—usually our mom. When he was gone, it was a great relief, and it was the only time we felt free in the truest sense of the word. But those times were so clouded with the anticipation of his return that we were held captive, whether he was there or not.

Mom loved us, though I don't recall that she ever said so. In her struggle to survive, she never once complained or abandoned her physical duties as wife and mother. Somehow, she carried on and kept us all together, even while she worked full-time at the factory.

In order to do this, she had to abandon her own needs and wants, had to abandon her very self. She gave up all her rights as a person and spent herself to meet her husband's every need and demand.

I'm sure she didn't see it that way. She could not have understood that, as she abandoned herself and her own feelings, she also lost the emotional capacity to connect with us. Anyone who observed her faithful presence and care might wonder how one of her children could claim that she had abandoned them. How could I dare make such a claim? Even *I* have found it confusing to untangle the threads of my experience and sort through what it all meant. Mom had abandoned us emotionally, and in the emotional void, I felt "left" by her.

It has taken me years to understand why I felt disconnected from my mother, why my relationship with her was good but lacked something vital, why I knew she was a very caring person but felt that she was really not interested in my life, and why, as an adult, I looked forward to time with her but knew there were levels of relating we could never visit. When Mom blocked her own feelings, our emotional connection was severed, and we never again touched at that level. I never felt her feelings for me, though now I am sure they were there.

During a visit shortly before she died, I asked her why she was never concerned about me, even as a kid. She answered, "I knew you were strong and could handle things. I never worried about you." That response pierced through layers of accumulated angst and gripped my heart until I had to fight not to scream at her, "But how was I to know that! You never told me!"

It seems my mom had, unknowingly, excused herself from ever having to comfort me, and in so doing, left me without the emotional connection I so desperately needed.

Abandoned

Left in the wake of years gone by,
Like a ghost whose spirit had moved on,
The gray, vacant house stood quietly there
Like a lost old man
Knee-deep in weeds,
Fragile, wind-swept, alone.

Once, life had resided therein.
Maybe there was laughter
But no doubt, pain;
Broken, bent, and battered,
And now, abandoned.

This isolated place of yesteryear,
This lost and lifeless space,
Seemed to welcome us awkwardly,
Our arrival, unexpected.
No time to hide the pile of broken stone
Once firm to feet for entrance to its rooms.

Empty and uncared for
Ignored, unseen, untouched
These acres and this building
Seem so far beyond repair.
Now, we were there.

Life returned
But we would pay a price.
We always do
If we would be transformed.

PART II

TELLING STORIES

Chapter Five

WHY STORIES?

When I return to the area where I grew up, I see the old grocery store boarded up, the tiff mill dyke covered with trees where we use to walk to the main road, and the place where we waited for the school bus, now covered with bushes and trees. My grandmother's home place is an empty field, with no sign of her log cabin or the old elm tree.

Each of these holds a story or many stories that I still carry in my heart. Though the external environment has changed over these past seventy-plus years, I can still see it all. I walk the land where we once ran and played, and I feel the earth's breath. Her soil holds the roots of my life, begun there as a child, where weeds now run wild and the evening breeze whispers of stories longing to be told.

Storytelling has been the way of humans from the very beginning. It has carried our histories and created our cultures. Storytelling has taught us, motivated us, frightened us, attracted, and repulsed us. Stories have entertained and even distracted us from the realities we have found unbearable. We share our lives through stories and enter other lives through these doors that reveal what lies beyond in the deepest recesses of our hearts and souls.

Our everyday stories and dramas are seldom recognized, let alone appreciated. They are happenings that carry us through our days as we grapple with what life hands us, moment by moment.

Some seem sordid, some surreal, some too insignificant to recount. Sometimes we tell ourselves stories and imagine something to be what it may or may not be. We vilify and sanctify, without really knowing who or what or why. Often in the telling of our story, we relive our pain and vulnerability and maybe release the tears we had not allowed to flow before. This is the price we sometimes pay for connecting and healing.

Stories are an effective way to pass on wisdom and values, since we can wrap them in images that are more easily remembered. Often we can identify with a situation more readily as we listen to a story, and thus open ourselves to receive the message at a deeper level where we can be touched and even transformed. In that open space of receptivity, the truth can access us, be absorbed and become a part of us without our even suspecting its arrival.

I have often found that in the very telling of my story, I hear something for the first time, or perhaps I hear it at a deeper level of understanding that heightens my awareness of some aspect of my experience I had not seen before. This happened many times during therapy sessions as I tried to make sense out of a childhood shortened by the trauma of emotional abandonment. I have come to understand that when my father emotionally and physically abused my mother, he not only stole her from my sisters and me but also from herself.

Everyone has a story waiting to be told. How sad to think that many will never be heard. Here, I offer only a few of the stories I have carried for a very long time.

As a small child, I told stories to my little sisters in the upstairs room of our battered house to distract us from what was happening to our mother downstairs. I was forced to make up stories when I had exhausted those I had learned from story books. I began to create characters and events that would entertain and grip their attention, even while I was, in those very moments, terrified of losing my mother.

The stories included here are all true and were written at various times in my life. Each one embodies something of me and my family's history and is therefore sacred and immutable. But even more, they are an expression of my effort to give a voice to the scared child that I was.

I also want to encourage other adult children who, like me, had no one to count on for comfort and no one to witness their experience, to discover hope for healing and transformation through the telling of their own stories.

Chapter Six

CAUGHT IN A STORM

They met at a church picnic, and she said it was love at first sight. It was one of those sultry August evenings, and I must have asked Mom how she and Daddy had gotten together.

Whatever my eight-year-old mind understood then, it could not have captured the full implications of what lay behind her smile as she told me the story of that day. I could only wonder what had happened to the man to whom she had given her heart.

How could she smile when she spoke of him? How could she still want to be with him? Surely she must be afraid of him. I was. Sometimes.

Some days there were no clouds, and the sky was a brilliant blue that promised everything joyous with lots of time to explore the woods and the creek. And then there were days when giant clouds rolled in and seemed to warn us of something on its way. The worst were the gray-black mounds of clouds that threatened the arrival of an outburst.

We had weathered many storms with my father at the center, exploding at something he didn't like. The words he hurled at Mom were like lightening strikes, the kind that could set fire to the dry summer grass. Sometime those mean words were shouted as he hit her. Afterward, she seemed so sad. And we never, never talked about it. If he had erupted suddenly, my sisters and I were silent witnesses to something we could not escape. All we could do was long for the relief that would come when the storm was over.

So we would return to our play as if nothing had happened. But it wasn't really play—at least not for me. I would simply go through the motions of whatever we were doing. But the storm raged on inside of me. I think I eventually walled it off in some chamber of my body, glad to be rid of it.

When I left home at age sixteen, I thought I had left it all behind. I don't recall thinking, "good riddance," but I do remember the profound relief I felt for a long time as I settled into living free of the abuse my father so readily heaped upon my mom. I eased my guilt for abandoning her and my younger sisters by paying off some of the family bills that were outstanding.

Now, years later, as I re-visit those painful times of long ago to tell my story of abandonment, I find some bits of that buried "storm energy" still lingering where I stored it all those years ago, still waiting to be resolved and released. The storm isn't raging like before, but it's definitely not over.

Chapter Seven

LOST

I walked away. The sounds were too painful. The words assaulted more than my mother. They vibrated through to my bones, so it took a while for me to escape them. The dark woods behind the house did not frighten me nearly so much. In fact, I felt embraced and welcomed into the cool fragrant space inhabited by bees and foxes and timid deer.

By now the echo of my father's voice faded, and I could think about something else. It wasn't hard to get lost in this lonely but beautiful space. In the stillness, I could hear my heart beat to the rhythm of the sounds of nectar-seeking bees and breeze-blown leaves. I stood for some time, eyes closed, feeling caressed. For this moment I felt safe.

I never knew exactly what I was looking for when I followed an abandoned path or looked under a rock or peered into the little stream that flowed nearby. I needed something, something beautiful, something to help me forget what was happening at my house. I needed to forget that I had left my mom when she needed me most. But I felt afraid and helpless. Maybe if I tried to interfere, it would make things worse. Maybe I had done something that had caused my father's rage. But I couldn't imagine what it was.

Just as I didn't know where I was going as I shuffled through the decaying leaves, I had no idea when to turn back, when it would be safe to return home. These were the thoughts that flittered in and out of my mind like the birds seeking night refuge in the branches above me. By now the sun was beginning to sink into the horizon. I had a strong need to distance myself from the blows and cruel words. Just as strong was the conflict within me, knowing that I had left not only my mom, but also my little sisters who were just one and five years old. I wasn't sure where they were when I left the house. Usually I did everything I could to protect them, sometimes taking them to play at the pond. But today I just left and didn't go to find them. And now, I needed to forget this terrible thing that I had done.

I walked deeper into the woods, always going in a straight line so that I could find my way home. I don't think I ever thought about continuing to walk and never turning back. I'm not sure why it never occurred to me to run away. But it didn't. I always went back. The same way my father always came home, no matter how late. So often, I prayed that he would not come home. But I knew he would be back, and it would start all over again.

On this day, I found a deep green bed of moss covering flattened rocks, as though someone had deliberately spread a soft carpet for me to sit on. Its beauty made me gasp with surprise and awe. I knelt and touched it, and it was cool and alive. I could feel its aliveness, and my fingertips tingled with delight. Almost afraid to crush its greenness, I sat down very carefully. Don't ask me how long I sat there. I didn't want to leave the comfort I had found. At some point I would start back. I knew Mom would worry that I was lost. I couldn't get lost. That would be one more burden she must not have.

Lost

Where did you go my little one
To what great depths did you descend
So that I could no longer hear your cry
Nor see the fading smile
The cringe
Where did you go?

I lost you somewhere along the way
I lost the chance to run and play.
I've come to find you little one.
I've come to learn again to Be.
Come sit beside me on this stone
Come, little one, and be with me.

I want to see
And hear and feel
I need to learn
How to be real.

Chapter Eight

INVISIBLE

September never came fast enough. Whether it was the autumn colors and piles of leaves other children romped in, new lessons and fresh-smelling books, or the escape from the chaotic unpredictability of home, I longed to return to school at summer's end.

At age five, I made my first journey away from home to start first grade, which is when I learned to read. Whole new worlds opened up to me through the magic of words, and like keys, they unlocked hidden rooms and allowed me to wander through ancient castles of discovery, as easily as walking a path in the woods.

Despite these wonders, the social experience of school was a painful struggle for me. I remember scrunching down in my seat when Sister Marie asked questions about something she had written on the chalkboard. My entire body cringed when I heard my name called. Not because I didn't know the answer. I almost always did. But I didn't like hearing my name. I was a bad person that nobody could like. Being singled out was so threatening to me that my heart would hammer in my chest. I was sure everyone could hear it.

I don't recall ever raising my hand in class. From the comments Sister Marie wrote on my papers, it was obvious that she was aware that I knew the answers. (Years later, one of my college professors would pen in big red letters on a paper he had marked with an A+, "You know this so well. Why don't you share it with the class?")

As my intellectual capacity increased, I preferred to hide somewhere with a book. When the other children ran with delight to the playground at recess, I lagged behind. They invaded the swing set, and I turned and ran to the church building, hopeful that no one had seen me. I enjoyed the coolness that welcomed me in from the summer heat. That vast space, the lingering fragrance of incense and burning candles, calmed me and embraced me.

I always sat in the front pew to be as close to God as possible. Sometimes I talked to him, but mostly I just sat there. I didn't mind that he looked at me. I believed that God knew what was inside of me. Here, I felt safe from everyone. No one ever came looking for me. No one ever asked where I had been. I knew they had not missed me, and that meant I could come back again.

There were times when I did go to the playground, but I never volunteered to play a game. The other children had to drag me in. I was always afraid that I would make a mistake, that I would do it wrong. So many times my father told me that I "couldn't do anything right," and I believed him. I couldn't wait for the game to be over, and all I thought about was how I might escape without anyone noticing. This worry was interspersed with my worry about going home after school, not knowing what to expect. There, in that chaos, I could not be invisible.

Unseen, Even By Me

Along a beaten path I strode
Where horse and rider often rode.
The silent trees beheld me there
And smiled, their branches glad to share.
Their shadows bid me safely be
Where I could sit and no one see
The tears and sadness buried deep,
Invisible now and mine to keep.
Invisible now, beyond my reach
What pain comes now, my walls to breach?

Chapter Nine

MY FIRST STAGE APPEARANCE

When I was eight years old, my heart started beating with excitement—something I seldom experienced—but my excitement was quickly doused by overwhelming anxiety. To my amazement, I had been chosen to be Little Bo Peep in the school play. Though I had never been in a play, a shaky thrill was bubbling up like a spring from some unknown part of me. I really wanted to do this, though I was also afraid of what it might mean.

Sister Bridget patiently explained to me what I needed to play the part. Holding the familiar storybook, she showed me what my dress should look like. Then she pointed to the shepherd's staff and said I needed to tie a large red bow around it. The bonnet must have a wide brim and needed to tie under my chin. And, oh yes, my hair needed to be arranged in long, banana curls. She touched the long, straight strands that hung down my back and seemed to question their potential for curls.

I would have no problem memorizing the lines of the nursery rhyme, but I wondered where I would get all these other things. As for the curls, my hair had never shown signs of curling. That was a bigger problem.

My Aunt Dorothy, who was one of those "take-charge" people, ran the school cafeteria and monitored my every move as I passed through the line with my tray. She always seemed to know how much food I needed, and I never objected. Apparently, Sister Bridget had spoken to her about what I needed for the play, and before I knew it, she was handling the whole matter. She said she would even find a classmate who could loan me a dress. But nothing was said about the curls.

For days, I mulled over what to do about my hair. How could I possibly tell my mom that I needed my hair done in banana curls? She might not know how to do it. I really didn't want to put another burden on her; there was so much tension at home already. So one day, without another thought, I decided I was not going to tell her. Of course, that created another problem. What would happen when I showed up for the play without the curls?

At some point I could no longer contain my excitement and knew I must tell Mom about the play. On that day, I arrived home and found her in the kitchen bent over the biscuit dough. She didn't say anything but looked up at me with a tired smile. I felt the heaviness. I knew she was worried, probably about everything. I sat my school bag down and sat on the kitchen chair nearest her. I watched her intently. I watched her cut the dough with a jelly glass, one we had collected from buying grape jelly. I watched her turn each soft, rounded biscuit in melted bacon grease and arrange it with the others in the battered bread pan. I was lost in watching the way she prepared biscuits, though I had seen her worn hands do this routine many times. "Helen, after you set the table, will you call the girls in for supper?"

I pushed my worry about the curls back, away from me and from Mom. That night I started to practice the lines I would recite in the play.

One day, when I worked with Mom out in the yard, I gathered the courage to tell her about the play and my part in it. She seemed pleased and smiled brightly. I told her she didn't have to worry about anything since Aunt Dorothy was taking care of everything I needed for the play. Later, when we finished the yard work, she helped me with my lines.

As the day got closer, I became more concerned. But again, I felt that little glimmer of excitement I had noticed when I was chosen for the part. This was a new feeling for me, to be chosen.

And then it arrived, that fateful day. I remember how nervous Mom seemed as she fussed with my dress and the bonnet Aunt Dorothy had provided. When it was time to leave, my father announced that he wasn't going. That familiar feeling of being threatened and then trapped grabbed at me as his words pounded in my ears.

My heart sank. My eyes filled with tears, and it felt like my life was ending. Mom didn't know how to drive. Only he could get us there. This meant that we would not get to the play. I would let my teacher and my classmates down. Suddenly the curls didn't matter. I had been tossed into a river and had to figure out how to swim. The argument that followed whirled around me as I imagined Sister Bridget's fury when I failed to show up. And then, to my surprise, Mom insisted that he at least take us to the school.

Full of anger, he agreed to drive us there. A heavy silence filled the car. I felt like I was suffocating and couldn't wait to get there. Without a word, my dad dropped us off in front of the school building and sped off. Mom went into the auditorium to find a place to sit with my sisters, and I ran as fast as I could and arrived behind the curtains minutes before the play was to start.

By now, I was torn between worry and excitement. I still had to face Sister Bridget without the banana curls. But it didn't matter. I was here, and Mom would see me up on the stage. I was sure that every one of my classmates could hear my heart beating when I took my place in line as we awaited our turn to go on stage.

And there she was, Sister Bridget, scowling as she watched me slip into place. Then it happened just as I expected—the storm.

With that tone of voice so familiar to me, she scolded me for arriving late and said, "Why isn't your hair done right?" Shrinking inside, I lowered my eyes and did everything I could to hold back the flood of tears that threatened to burst forth. *Not now, I can't cry now! How could so much go so wrong when I wanted it all to work out?*

Even as I write this, there is a kind of sickening feeling in the pit of my stomach that radiates through my body. But more than that, I also feel a deep appreciation for what happened next.

This little girl Bo Peep, who had withstood a violent storm at home and at school, walked out on the stage and, for the first time ever, faced an auditorium packed with people, possibly a hundred or more. I remember how my legs threatened to melt as I scanned that blur of faces. At one point I looked for Mom but never found her. It was too scary to keep looking.

I caught my breath, stood straight, tall, and alone with my shepherd's staff in my right hand. I opened my mouth and waited for the words to come out. At first they were soft and hesitant, but then I swallowed hard and shouted, "Little Bo Peep has lost her sheep….and doesn't know where to find them."

We had to find a ride home that night because my father didn't come back for us. Once again, I felt a mixture of excitement and disappointment. Mom was quiet as we rode home with my Uncle Sim and his family, so I never knew what she thought of my performance. As for my dad, like so often before, he had succeeded in stealing the joy that I so hungered for.

Chapter Ten

THE ORCHARD KEEPER

I was only six when it started, or maybe that's when it got worse. I'm not sure. But I do remember where I was. I had spent most of the morning pulling weeds in the vegetable garden, which covered a large area of the slight hill that sloped down from the old house. The hill wasn't that steep, but you could get out of breath walking up it on a hot summer day.

The old pear tree that stood near the edge of the garden provided a little bit of shade, but it was gone by that time of day. I liked being in the garden, feeling the dust between my toes and touching the plants and watching them grow. My job was to keep the weeds from overgrowing the beans and tomatoes. It was peaceful there among the rows.

It was also hot, and I was really thirsty. I started to run up to the house to get a drink when I heard my dad shouting at Mom. I heard other noises, like things falling. I stopped by the old pear tree and hid behind its knotted trunk. I was glad that my two little sisters were over at Grandma's house. I was afraid for Mom. My heart beat so loudly that I could hardly think of what to do next, so I ran down to the orchard.

The orchard bore the markings of abandonment. It was a little further down the hill and off to the west side of the garden. I discovered it one day shortly after we moved in and felt sad when

I saw it. The trees looked old and bent, and they were surrounded by dead branches in the weeds. The grass grew wild and tall, so that you could barely see the lower part of the tree trunks. When there were apples, they were hard and bitter, but I ate them anyway. This spot was hidden from the house and garden. The trees must have been planted by someone because they stood in three straight lines. They seemed ready to march right down the hillside.

There was a wooden shack just on the edge of the old orchard that had one opening for a window and another for a doorway. The dirt floor was covered with dead leaves that had blown in, and something had made a nest in one corner of the tiny room. A little creek bed came out of the woods and passed right behind the shack. It was dry unless it rained, and then it ran off into a small pond.

As far as I know, no one else ever came down here, so it was my special place. I could sit on a tree limb and watch the bees humming through the honeysuckle that grew along the broken rail fence that stopped in the middle of a nearby field. Once I stayed long enough to finish my *Alice in Wonderland* book, and when I got back to the house, Mom scolded me for always having my nose in a book. I think she had been worried about me, though she never said.

Mom never said much to us, and she always looked worried. I knew she worried about Dad's drinking and not having enough money. Some mornings, after one of his rages, she would have a bruise on her arm or leg. I always wanted to ask her if she was okay, but I was afraid to say anything because she didn't seem to want to talk. So I thought it best to be quiet and pretend I didn't see it. But, oh, I did worry about her, even though she went on making breakfast as if nothing had happened.

When I needed to escape my dad's terrifying craziness, I went to the woods or the old orchard, my special place. The apple trees were always there, waiting for me with their arms outstretched.

The third tree in the second row seemed to call out to me. Her branches were low and easy to climb. Her trunk was large, knobby in places, smooth in others. My back fit right into one of the smooth places.

On this particular day, I climbed up several branches to where I could lean against her trunk, and sat for a long time. I was so mad at my dad. *How could he do this? Why did he do it? Mom takes such good care of us, making meals and scrubbing our clothes and taking care of the garden and the chickens. She didn't do anything to deserve this.* I couldn't understand any of it. I kicked the tree, again and again. I leaned into her trunk and cried until my chest ached. *Why does she put up with this? Why doesn't she take us away from him? Why? What will we do if he kills her?*

When I stopped crying, I felt bad that I had kicked my tree. "I'm sorry," I said to the old apple tree. I've talked to other trees before, and they always seem to say something back to me. I could hear her say, *It's okay, Helen. I know you're upset.* As I pressed against her trunk, she continued to hold me on her old but strong branch.

I was so overwhelmed by the feeling that I needed to make up for kicking her so violently that I slid down from her arms into the tall weeds that hugged her trunk. *I know what I can do*, I thought, as the weeds enveloped me. With both my hands wrapped tightly around their invading blades, I tugged until their roots let go of the soil and landed on my butt. I worked quickly until the tree was free, with a clear space surrounding her. My hands were dirty and bleeding, but I felt I had returned her kindness. It was beginning to get dark, and I picked up fallen twigs and piled them with the weeds near the edge of the orchard. On the way back to the house, I stopped to listen. All was quiet, except for the call of a mourning dove.

That summer, I returned to the old orchard often to sit in my tree and feel her comforting presence. I always felt welcomed and accepted. It was a safe place for me to be with my anger and sadness about what was happening in my home. Sometimes the wind blew through her leaves, and she seemed to whisper: *I'm so glad you came, Helen. I will hold you as long as you want to stay.*

I did feel safe, like I belonged there. *I'm so glad you are here—has it been a long time? I mean, have you always been here? When it storms, does it scare you? You have no place to go.*

When a mourning dove lit on a nearby branch and rustled the leaves, it seemed like a smile. *You are full of questions today. Did a storm bring you here? Are you afraid?*

I really did wonder how long she had been there and what it was like for her to be without protection. *Yes, I am afraid. My dad is being mean again. I don't know what to do. So I came here where it's quiet, where I feel protected, at least for a while.* Her leafy arm dipped in the afternoon breeze and touched my face.

I've been here a long time, Helen, through many storms, cold winters, and insect attacks. It hasn't been easy, but bending in the wind, holding on, and sometimes letting go has made me strong over the years. That will happen for you, too.

Though I didn't realize it then, the orchard and I had a lot in common: we were both without the attention we needed, abandoned, and in some ways, weren't being cared for. Maybe this is why I worked so hard that summer to keep the weeds and grass in check, using the rusty sickle that hung on a nail in the old shed. It was so little to do for this brave tree and all the others that were there for me, despite their own struggles. They seemed so strong and they never gave up.

> *It wasn't enough to survive. It was necessary to look at the past and find meaning in it.*
>
> —Mary Fahy
> *The Tree That Survived the Winter*

Solace

Do you remember when you began to hide?
First your body
Then your heart.
Do you remember when you found a space
Where you could not hide,
Did not want to.
A place where you were free to Be
The little creek
The old orchard and the trees
The fields of Queen Anne's Lace
You were so small
The weeds so tall
Through them you made your path
To sounds that called
And watched the croaking frog dive in
And float away
To hidden depths
You learned to delve
In the solace of those solitary hours.

Chapter Eleven

MY FIRST BEST FRIEND

The soft mud was soothing as it squished between my toes. The splash of raindrops on my face laughed at my dripping hair. I smiled back and grabbed at falling raindrops. The wet grass wrapped itself around my legs as I wandered through the meadow near Grandma's house. Like the gray clouds above, I was in no hurry. The hot, dry earth enjoyed the rain shower as much as I did. It was long overdue.

My secret friend, the little creek, seemed happy with the water as it flowed through her banks, down from the nearby hillside. She had been dry for weeks, so we could not play until now. I would stay for a while.

We were friends, this little creek and me. Her water was now deep enough for me to dip my toes, so I sat down on the bank and let the water gurgle past my ankles as we reacquainted ourselves.

In some spots, she bubbled over the rocks that passing feet had edged into her creek bed. Those stones, worn smooth by many seasons of her flow, created a muffled sound, while others, with still jagged edges, created a musical sound as they teased the flowing water. Larger stones impeded the water, blocking the flow only to release it. The sounds the water made as it tumbled beyond the blockages was the most beautiful of all music, full of joy and merriment.

I sat for a long time and listened to what she had to say, and I was sure that no one but me could interpret her beautiful language. *I've missed you, Helen. Are you glad I'm back?*

Oh, yes, little creek. I've waited for this day and your coolness and your song. I knew you would return. I have so much to tell you about school and home and my dad—especially about him, though I really don't want to talk about it. She caressed my feet and sang to me with her bubbly flow. Her sound and touch invited me to touch her.

I dipped both my hot hands into her gurgling stream and splashed with all my might. She giggled with delight and said, *Oh, let's play!*

With that, I began to gather larger rocks and place them across the little creek, from one side to the other. Then I packed the empty spaces between with mud that was plentiful along the bank. The water backed up into a little pool, but only for a while. When it was full, she slid beyond the barrier, laughing as she flowed past me.

I leaned over to look down into the water and saw that she had captured the clouds and the tree branches—and my straggly hair, still wet from the rain. In time, the mud washed away and once again, the water flowed defiantly through the little rock dam I had constructed.

I loved it here in the silence, where only the voice of the water and the sound of crickets and croaking frogs spoke of a secret, mysterious life that went on unnoticed by all but me. There was never a time when my little friend didn't welcome me to sit beside her. She liked it when I dropped in pebbles and watched the ripples dance across her surface. Never a complaint. And when she was a dry little creek bed, she seemed desolate at not being able to offer me her soothing touch and gurgling smile.

When the world seemed to reject me, when there were few places to hide from my father's anger, when no one seemed to understand how I felt, this was one of the places I returned to. My tears were often swept away by the torrents of this little creek that knew only how to play.

Sometimes, after my pain was silenced by her gentle murmur, I would sit with my hand dangling in her coolness and let my thoughts wander out over the field off in the distance. I would wonder how she could be so happy when I felt so alone and sad. I wanted so much to be like everyone else—including her. I wanted to do the things the other kids seemed to do with such fun and ease.

One day, I asked my friend, the little creek, if there was something wrong with me, but she only smiled, welcomed me, and treated me like her best friend. I wonder if she felt my longing for the freedom to be like the other kids—to laugh and play and lose myself in games that seemed to entertain them for hours on end. I could not do that. And because of the pain of my separation, I often slipped away when no one was looking (and felt guilty about leaving). It was so painful. I wanted to be part of the group, but because of my fears, I wasn't able.

Many seasons with their droughts and eventual downpours passed before I came to grips with the isolation and fear that held me back from life. It was only after I left the fields, my little friend the creek, and the secret hiding places of my childhood that I entered into the stream of life—my life—and came to know the beauty that had been growing inside me all along.

As I write this, I realize that I was conscious only of the mysteries going on all around me during those warm and sometimes wet summer days of the 1940s. Reflecting back on those solitary moments now, I suspect that there was a whole other set of "life happenings" going on inside of me at the time—so deep and so real that I am only now beginning to get in touch with them. I want to touch them, feel them, taste them, because I know there is something very beautiful inside me flowing from those moments alone with my friend, the little creek.

I fully realize that the child befriended by the little creek still exists inside me. She is very gentle, taught well by her flowing friend on those rainy, summer days. She still longs for the silent escape to those hidden moments and sometimes fears the intrusions of life's harshness. But this child is also accompanied by the woman she eventually released, filled with the longing to drink deep of life and all it offers.

My first best friend taught me much that I will never forget and more that I am still learning. She is gone from the landscape of my grandmother's property now, but returns at times in my fondest memories. When I recall her comforting presence, I also sense the bubbly, playful, carefree way she streamed along her time-worn path. The rocks that might have been obstacles slowed her down a bit, but only briefly. As she found another way around them, her watery arms embraced them and made music that touched deep into my heart. On she went, slowing down at the bends in her banks and dropping over the rocks, down from some secret place in the hills. She wound her way along her path and eventually reached a larger creek some miles away, but not before she had wound her way through my heart.

Life has its mysteries. Some slip past us, but not without our learning something through their presence. I could never tell you all that I learned, sitting there in the coolness of the little creek. Yet, I know with certainty the meaning and beauty of friendship, of singing and silent comforting, and of dancing in the sun because she gave me these gifts of her life.

Now and then I long for a creek to sit beside and to lose myself in its flow. Someday I'll write more about the lessons I learned at her side. Someday I'll write about friendship.

In The Silence Of My Soul

I wander down to the little creek
And sit
In the silence of my soul
Where only the clouds go passing by
In the surface of the stream.

The sun is just rising from her rest
The dove and the lark remain in their nest
And my heart surrenders to the approaching light
That awakens its dreams
And puts them to flight.

The flow of the creek seems to know where to go
The bird on the wing seems to know what to sing

But I for a time must wait in the flow
For direction revealed in the moments that go
Through the days of my life
Moving ever so slow.
One day I will know

What is real
What is not

As the light lifts the darkness
And the shadows dance off
And the lark leads the singing
In the silence of my soul.

Chapter Twelve

THE TREE

I have cherished my relationship with trees since childhood. I think it began around age five when we moved in with my paternal grandparents. I had just started first grade, and when I learned to read, it threw open doors to explore places beyond my own world. My imagination was set free like a horse running wild.

I escaped my father's scary behavior by exploring nature, where I could lose myself in what she had to offer: the old orchard, the fields, the little creek, the woods. There were endless places to explore in the woods, where the ground was carpeted with years of fallen leaves and patches of wild flowers and strange rock formations. And there was one special tree that stood outside the woods, a few yards down in front of my dad's mom's log cabin. We called it "The Old Elm Tree."

Her leafy branches spread out several yards from her enormous trunk, and she was much taller than the house or the barn. Here, under her thick shade, I built my first play house. I imagined a living space of my own design and created it with rocks I gathered from the nearby creek. I arranged them carefully to form the walls of rooms—bedrooms, living room, hallway, kitchen. I left openings in the rows of rocks to form the doorways and windows. Within these boundaries I played with imaginary characters, careful not to step over the stones but to walk through the doorways.

Each summer when I returned to Grandma's place, I spent most of my free time under her tree, where I could daydream and expand my imagination. When I entered this space, it was like being with an old friend who was always waiting there for me.

This was no ordinary tree, the one that stood in all her elegance in front of Grandma's house, just a little south of the area she called her yard. Since her yard stretched out into a field, Grandma had planted bushes that burst full of little pink roses in the summer. These, along with an assortment of other flowering plants, provided a boundary that embraced the area nearest the house, an old log cabin whose long history has been lost to those of us who remain.

Sometime in my forties, I returned to the old homestead to visit an aunt who lived just up the hill from where Grandma had lived. I looked forward to walking down to visit my tree after years of being gone from home. Standing at the crest of the hill behind my aunt's house, I was shocked to find an expansive spread of gently sloping space, green but empty. Not only was the house, the smokehouse, and the barn gone, but there was no visible evidence of the great old tree that had adopted and nurtured me all those years ago, not even a stump that I could go sit on and reminisce.

I remember that day well. The rolling thunder and gray clouds threatened to envelop me, and a resounding wave of dreadful sadness wrenched at my roots. I was flooded with images of time spent in that house and the endless hours lived out under the old elm tree.

How strange. As I looked into that empty space, I could see the vast torso that I had leaned against on those hot summer days. I could feel the rough bark of her trunk, so gigantic that an adult with arms long enough to wrap around her could not begin to touch their own fingers. I saw myself sitting on her gnarled roots that seemed to resist submergence beneath the tree. They dipped into the ground at some points and then rose up and curled around the base of the tree. I have never seen anything like it since. I could literally sit in the spaces created by the winding roots, shaped like arms that could hold me. My small body did often rest in those welcoming arms, soaking in the warmth of her energy. I wonder how she felt as she held this sad child who seldom smiled. Did she feel the aloneness and the sadness that often brought me to her? Did she know the confusion and fear that overwhelmed me during those years of my father's cruel abuse toward my mother?

This great old tree mothered me during those summer days when Mom worked at the factory and seldom had the energy to hold me or talk with me. I worried about Mom. My sisters and I would walk across the fields in the early morning hours to stay with Grandma, where I usually occupied myself alone under the elm tree. I'm not sure where my sisters were during those moments, probably in the house with Grandma.

Her leafy branches were so thick, not a ray of sun could pierce them. Sometimes I would sit in Grandma's wheelbarrow, its handles firmly rooted on the ground, and soak in the coolness. The humming of bees was the background melody as I looked up into her leaves and counted them until I ran out of numbers. It would eventually rain and drench the dry, dusty path that meandered past the tree, but not a drop dampened my special space. And on summer nights when the moon and the stars shone so bright that I could read my school book outside, I would leave her embracing shadow to stand under the sky lights and count the stars. In the fall, when she was leafless, I looked up through her branches to watch the clouds as they morphed into every animal I could imagine.

I could write volumes about my mothering tree. Even now, I feel such gratitude for her presence in my child life, which gave me more than shade. My tree was always there, always welcoming and embracing me with the safety and solace I did not feel at home. I could never understand my father's behavior, his explosions caused by nothing that I could see, his cruelty toward my mom and sometimes to us kids. When I was terrified that he might kill my mother, I found a place deep inside me to hide my fear and told no one. But when I went to be near my tree the next day, all that scary stuff melted away as I rearranged the rocks of my playhouse. Sometimes in those hours, the memory of the night before would return. I would sit on her roots, lean into her bark, and stare at the rolling field just beyond, where the creek crawled lazily past the gooseberry bushes.

As I stood on the crest of the hill, the clouds that had threatened now dumped rain in small droplets and brought me out of my reverie. I realized that everything that had once filled that empty space was not really gone. It was only my eyes that could not see it. My heart still carried those childhood moments, the tree and all her embraces.

Because of my connection with my tree, I somehow survived the terror of those days gone by. She became a strong character in my life, one that allowed me to imagine and develop an inner dialogue that would eventually provide a strong resource for my own growth and development. My relationship with her is one that cannot be cut down or dismissed, so deeply rooted is she in my very being. Her tree-ness, now breathing through me, has not only nurtured and helped heal this emotionally abandoned child but has taught me that sometimes we find what we need in the most surprising places.

Under The Elm Tree

I look up past her thick, green leaves,
Into a deep blue canopy.
A beam of sunshine peeking through,
Teases me.

I lean back in the rusty old wheelbarrow,
My feet planted on the dry summer ground,
Face lifted to the crowded, cloud-filled sky.
I count the elephants passing by.

I sit on the up-reaching root of the tree.
Its rough bark scratches my legs—but I stay
And lean against her sturdy trunk,
Dreaming of distant places I'll go someday.

I gather rocks from the creek nearby.
A pile, they tumble at my feet.
Carefully I arrange them according to the picture in my head,
Each square, a room of the house I'll one day build.

And so passes the hours of my lonely days,
Shaded from the hot sun's rays
Protected for a while, from the pain
to which I must return.

The Surrogate

There was a tree
That mothered me.
She gave her all
As I recall…

Her shade
Her strength
Her silent watch
Embraced and nurtured me.

The spot where she once stood
Is bare.
Yet, I cannot forget her care,
The way that she was always there,
Her arms reaching out to welcome me,
My Grandmother's ancient elm tree.

Chapter Thirteen

I WILL PLANT COSMOS

Once when I was driving through the state of Virginia, I noticed a blur of crimson spread over a large area along the road. I felt the urge to stop and discover what it was. To my delight, I walked into a field of flowering cosmos, and something felt strangely familiar.

It's true. I have always smiled when I saw a bed of cosmos. The purple and white ones are my favorites, and now I learned that they could be crimson, too. Why this particular flower caught my attention and triggered such a sense of wanting to be near them was a mystery to me. Then one sunny day, I looked into the upturned faces of a bouquet of these blossoms at the market, and I remembered something.

The very large vegetable garden that used to hold us captive with weeding and hoeing on those hot childhood days always had one corner with no vegetables. Mom reserved the northeast corner of the plot for her flower bed. The rainbow of pink, red, and white rose moss crouched in front like children in an old family photo. The orange and yellow zinnias stood just behind as if they were the young adults. In the back row, the stately cosmos towered over them all, the seniors of the family. The fern-like greenery held high their smiling faces.

One day, years later after discovering the crimson cosmos, I asked my aging mother about her flowerbed, why she always grew those particular plants. She smiled and traveled back in time, show-ing me a little girl who had received a handful of seeds from her mom. She had eagerly planted them along a path in the yard and checked them frequently to see what would show up.

Eventually they grew, budded, and blossomed into rose moss, zinnias, and cosmos. Since then, she looked forward to welcom-ing them back each year. Perhaps this was her only bit of beauty during those cruel years of my father's abuse. How wonderful that she persisted in creating this patch of beauty for herself, as if to say defiantly to all of us, "I will plant my cosmos; I will have some beauty in my life."

Eventually, Mom left us. She outlived my father by twenty-three years, and during that time, she blossomed as she got her life back. Forty years of emotional and physical abuse had not destroyed her spirit. Nor had it lessened her zest for life and her love of plants, which she passed on to me and my sisters.

Recently my sister, Carol, sent me a note card that contained two packets of cosmos seeds. She knew that I had not been able to find any that spring. I bought a pot and potting soil. I declared that day a holiday and celebrated by honoring my mom's tradi-tion. I planted cosmos.

Cosmos

Great Space, O loving Universe,
Resplendent with stars and planets that light up the night sky,
Have you met the plant that bears your name?
Do you know from whence she came?
In all her regal graciousness
She holds her head of loveliness
Above leafy arms in readiness
To gift us with her tenderness.
Her gentle bending in the wind
Betrays her strength for weathering
The worst of storms.
Fresh face finding sun
Lifting blossoms, having fun
Cosmos dancing in the rain
I remember you
And plant you once again.

PART III

THE INNER JOURNEY
OF THE EMOTIONALLY
ABANDONED CHILD

Chapter Fourteen

MY INNER WORLD:
A CLOSER LOOK AT THE
CHILD'S PERSPECTIVE

I n his book, *When Dad Hurts Mom: Helping Your Children Heal the Wounds of Witnessing Abuse*, author Lundy Bancroft identifies five key concepts in the child's experience of living with family violence. He describes what goes on in the inner world of the child, and these concepts are the basis of this chapter. A child's inner world is a wondrous place of make-believe, magic, wonder, and discovery. However, if her outer space is filled with trauma, the child's inner world may be cluttered with confusion, fear, insecurity, guilt, shame, and a poor sense of self.

Concept #1 – Children are aware of the abuse.

Even at the ages of five and six, I was acutely aware of what was going on, especially when it affected my mother. This awareness never left me. Whether it was happening at the time or had happened three days or three months earlier, what I witnessed followed me like a dense fog that enveloped me. The sense of an ever-present danger, the need to protect, the fear of someone I loved, and the worry about my mom fed my abiding vigilance and my heightened awareness.

My sisters and I were often silent witnesses to our father's abuse. We stood nearby and did not know what to do. He assailed her with the vilest of language and called her demeaning names; he slapped and pushed her, ignoring our presence. Sometimes we witnessed the abuse from another room and heard him physically attack her, and then heard her cry out. Both the visual and auditory experiences were painful for me and triggered feelings I could not begin to identify at the time, but fear was the worst of these emotions. Every fiber of my being was infused with fear, and fear was the place from which I approached life, even well into my forties.

The signs that my father had violently attacked Mom were visible. Though she tried to hide or ignore the impact on her, Mom's pain never escaped me. I saw the bruises, the swelling, the black eyes. I felt her sadness, her unexpressed anger, her fear. In her denial, she may have thought I did not notice. She never knew that everywhere I went, I carried with me the images of the blows, the words, and her cries.

The atmosphere in our home could be heavy or sullen, even on a sunny day. It was often quiet. I didn't feel safe enough to say anything about anything. Most of what I felt in my childhood went unspoken, left to smolder within the inner workings of my mind and heart. No one ever noticed my worry and confusion, and I never shared it with anyone, least of all, Mom. I would not add anything more to her burden. The tragedy of all of this was not just what she bore and what I carried—much worse was the fact that, caught in my inner world, I could never connect with her in a way that let her know how much she meant to me, and certainly I failed to feel that I meant anything to her. So little passed between us.

Concept #2 – Children's interpretations can matter as much as their experiences.

When it came to interpreting my experience, I focused on the physical damage that was done to our mom, and sometimes to the room where it occurred. I had no understanding of the emotional damage that was being inflicted on all of us. Nor did I understand that, because of how I interpreted what was happening, my sense of self was being diminished. I had no framework for interpretation other than my own, which was completely inadequate.

For example, Mom never made reference to the abuse; she never spoke of it. She remained silent. She never complained about what was happening, even when she was physically injured. I interpreted her silence to say: This is not to be talked about, to anyone, ever. My sisters and I never talked about it as children, and we never spoke of it as adults until recent years. It was as though we had an unspoken agreement, a secrecy bond that held us hostage to our shared memories. Perhaps we did not want to revisit the cruel pain; it was enough to have endured it.

While I felt a deep loneliness from not talking about the situation, I also longed for someone with whom I could connect. We lived in a rural area where people mainly saw each other on Sundays at church or when they stopped by one of the local taverns. Our nearest neighbors were several miles away, but my experience of isolation went far beyond this physical separation from others.

One of the most significant interpretations that impacted my life was my belief that my mother was not interested in me. During those preschool years while my father was away with the military, she played with us, sang to us, made our dresses, and gave us lots of attention. When he returned, the abuse began, and she seemed to have no time for us. I don't recall her ever asking about my day at school, what I did, or how it was going. I remember there were things I wanted to tell her about, like the day I fell off the playground slide and the day I found out I was going to be Little Bo Peep in the school play.

As an adult, with the help of a psychotherapist, I spent hours re-interpreting what either happened or didn't happen between my mother and me. I now see it from a different framework, and

I appreciate the fact that she maintained our household, worried about where the money would come from to pay the bills, and kept us fed, clothed, and in school. I've also worked through my anger that Mom did not protect us, that she didn't take us away from this cruel person. Even as an adult, I could not make sense of this until I began working with abused women. I now understand that they have multiple reasons for staying.

With no one to talk to about our situation, I learned early on to figure things out for myself, whether it was about what went on at home or the other challenges in my life. I became convinced that my concerns weren't that important. The skills I developed for coping with life were limited, but somehow they got me through. However, they were fear-based and created countless problems for me as I grew into adolescence and young adulthood.

My primary interpretation of life was one of fear, of survival, and of being careful not to "cause" another person to become angry. My own anger began to emerge during my adolescent years. It reached its peak in my early forties, at which time I was forced to confront those years of accumulated anger, anger that had covered the fear.

Concept #3 – The children are frightened.

Whether my father was drinking or not, he got what he wanted by instilling fear in us and then showing us what he was capable of doing if we failed to comply. Of course, if he was drunk, it was always worse. His very presence embodied the threat of violence, which is how he controlled us. Every day I lived with the belief that, one day, he would kill my mom and then us. We lived in an isolated area, several miles from the nearest neighbor. There were no telephones, no way to call for help, no way to get away from the danger. When he did not come home after work, which frequently happened, I prayed that he would never come home—a prayer that went unanswered. He always returned, often late at night.

The trepidation preceded him. Shortly before it was time for him to come home, a dark cloud moved in and shrouded everything, and a sick feeling formed in the pit of my stomach. I never knew what to expect but always anticipated the worst. Most of the time he arrived sullen, argumentative, demanding, and verbally abusive. But there were also times when nothing happened. The unpredictability always kept me wary, and in this state, I developed a keen sense of watchfulness and was sensitive to Mom's demeanor, which was difficult to read. She usually hid her feelings with a blank look that revealed nothing of her pain.

Within the confines of my fear, I was always on the alert, always thinking about what to do next. "What if" became my fixed perspective. I was always preoccupied with worry about something. Most of all, I worried about Mom. Early on, I was out of touch with my anger that she did not take us away from this situation. That came later. At this early age, my focus was on the fear that Mom would be killed and we would be next or the fear of what would happen to us if he killed her.

At the same time, I did not want to add to her burden, so I never told her of my fears. I never talked about the things that worried me, perhaps in some part because I did not have the words to do so. Mostly, I remember not wanting to make things more difficult for her. If I needed something, I would first try to work it out myself, and then go to her reluctantly, only if I could not resolve it. I learned to do without and eventually found comfort in being able to handle situations myself.

Whenever I was overwhelmed with fear and worry, I went into the woods. There, amidst the trees and brushwood, I felt safe and welcomed. There all my fears and worries were replaced with the wonder of it all. When I walked in the wet weeds after the rain or followed a path into a sunlit meadow, I could be a child, lost in wonder, curious, and amazed at what I discovered. I would play in the creek, damming up the water to watch it find a way around the rocks. Or I would pile rocks up in the shape of a little shrine and kneel there to pray. How does a child of five or six pray? For me, as I recall, there often were no words. I would simply kneel or sit there on the cool, green moss and know that I was safe for that moment. It was then that God seemed close enough to put his arms around me, something that I longed for.

Mom was not a person who showed affection. I do not remember her hugging us. I mostly remember her as being busy with keeping the household together. She was a good cook. I spent hours just watching her prepare meals, cutting biscuits with a drinking glass, peeling potatoes, flouring pieces of chicken. I helped her hang clothes on the line outside and helped clean the house. These were safe moments when my father was usually not around.

My favorite time was working with her in the garden where she had her corner planted with zinnias, cosmos, gladiolas, and rose moss. Here, amongst the vibrant colors and weed-pulling, my fears seemed to melt away from me—perhaps from her, too. We rarely spoke. I recall very few conversations with my mother. Consequently, I never really got to know her.

I only knew my fear, and that walled me into a very small world that Mom never entered.

Concept # 4 – Children believe they are to blame.

I don't recall ever thinking to myself, *This is my fault.* But I do recall the feeling of guilt that came from a belief deep inside me that I was bad and had done something to cause these awful things my dad was doing. If I did something different, maybe it would stop. In my child-mind, I did not know what that "something different" was. In the midst of the unpredictability and chaos in our family, I did feel some comfort when I was doing some form of cleaning. I could sweep the floor and make the bed and pick up trash in the yard.

Keeping things clean and in order became a need—indeed, an obsession with me. I perceived order and comfort as a way to make things better. It was, hopefully, a way to get rid of the chaos and unpredictability, a way to get my father to stop his brutal attacks. Of course, this never worked. What did happen was my mother's burden was lightened a bit, and it did feel good to see that I was helping her. Neither she nor I knew then that this seemingly desirable behavior covered up my deep feelings of guilt and anxiety. Insisting on order in my external world had become my way of coping with the very uncomfortable feelings that haunted me.

Guilt is a terribly heavy thing for anyone to carry, especially as a child. Understanding the dynamic between cause and effect is something that only happens as the child develops. Until then, the self-centeredness that characterizes infants, toddlers, and young children is the perspective from which they view their world. So it is that I saw myself as the cause of what occurred in my family, and I desperately wanted to fix it. When I couldn't effect any change, I carried the guilt of my failure.

I felt this same sense of guilt when I chose not to intervene when my father was hurting my mom. I carried that guilt into my forties, when I addressed it in therapy and realized that there had been valid reasons for me to withdraw in fear. My need for forgiveness, along with my distorted patterns of thinking, feeling, and behaving, haunted me well into adulthood and became the work of years of psychotherapy.

Concept #5 – Children want to talk about the abuse, but they feel that they can't.

The physical isolation I experienced living in a rural area was nothing compared to the emotional and social isolation. My choices at the time, which were rooted in fear, guilt, and shame, created some of this experience. My first impulse was to hide what was happening in my home. My father's dangerous behavior, my mother's inability to do anything about it and her resulting depression, and the poverty in which we lived were all reasons to never tell anyone about anything.

Further, bringing a classmate home from school was never a consideration. I dared not, since I never knew what condition my father would be in. I couldn't risk anyone finding out how things were in my home. In high school, I was even more determined that no friends would see my home. So that it would never become an issue, I chose not to get involved in anything at school. I didn't participate in any extracurricular activities, something I always felt bad about. Therefore, I was always on the outside looking in. In the end, I finished my school days as someone no one else knew, someone I didn't even know.

And so, it was all my secret, a heavy secret to carry. I never spoke of this to my mother or siblings. In my aloneness, I mulled over everything. I worried, especially about my mom. I secretly hoped that someone would discover our situation and rescue us from the monster in our home. I think I must have felt some sense of loyalty to the family beyond my self-imposed secrecy. No one had ever told me not to talk about it.

On the other hand, if someone had asked me about my home life, I think I would have denied it all. It was that bad. I needed to hide the shame and embarrassment and my own confusion about why my mother was being abused by my father, of all people.

This is not to say that I didn't want to talk about it, but where would I have found the words? Some of the words I needed had not yet been formed within me. Others were buried by pain, like acorns at summer's end, deep beneath layers of leaves left from years long spent. I didn't want anyone to know about the shame and guilt that I, myself, couldn't accept. I built a wall of denial that protected me, but also walled me off from myself.

Years later on a warm fall day, I sat in my room with memories flashing from thirty years past. I am not sure why, on this particular day, they pushed past the boundaries of my denial. Like the roar of a dragon escaping years of captivity, vibrations began to form deep within my chest cavity, eventually emerging as sounds that evolved into words, words that described what I had tried so hard to forget. As the words formed in my mouth, I wanted to run. Instead, I stayed, stunned by the awfulness of what I spoke aloud.

"My father beat my mom."

I cried, feeling the pain and the sadness that came from allowing this truth to surface after all these years. I cried for many reasons that day, but especially from the sense of freedom. At last, I was able to release my burden. As I spoke these words aloud to myself, I unlocked a door behind which my ugly truth and I had been prisoners.

It was years before I could trust enough to let anyone else look at what began on that warm, autumn day. I had broken the silence with myself, which charted the course to find my voice and make other painful admissions. The process of looking at and accepting what I had finally admitted to myself became quite disruptive. The truth of the abuse was like a spotlight that shined on multiple issues that had complicated my adult life, all of them rooted in the fear that had imprisoned me since childhood. However, it would be another six years before I could talk about the family violence, understand its impact, and begin to heal.

As a child who witnessed my mother's abuse, my inner world was a painful place to live. Though there is so much more that could be included here, I will share one more area that was a defining part of my experience. I felt shame, both for myself and for my family.

This child, the one who was me, had barely gotten started in life when my father began his regular abusive behavior. I felt shame and embarrassment about my situation, and ultimately, about who I was. I felt like a failure, unable to do anything to help my mom, a feeling that was affirmed by my father who told me again and again that I could do nothing right. He had to be right. He was my father. So I believed him.

These beliefs, along with my generalized fear and anxiety, formed my perception of who I was—that I was someone bad, that I was limited, unlovable, and undeserving of attention. I felt shame about myself, my situation, and my failure to do anything to change it.

My sense of shame always lurked around the corner of my awareness. Eventually, I became very aware that I wore only hand-me-downs, clothing from older cousins that seldom fit me and were always out of style. The clothes that Mom made for me demonstrated her total lack of skills as a seamstress, and when I wore them, my sense of shame and feeling "less than" everyone else only deepened.

My feelings of shame increased as I grew older, and I remember an incident that has haunted me for years, something for which I have struggled to forgive myself. I was probably in sixth or seventh grade. Money was always sparse, and I knew Mom worried about this. So did I. Mom was someone who did without so that we could have more. She rarely, if ever, bought anything for herself, making do with what she had, and frankly, some of her clothing was really shabby.

I don't know why this bothered me so much at that early age, but I do know that I was so ashamed of her dress one Sunday that I wouldn't sit with her in church. From that time on, I found another place to sit. I was acutely aware of why I chose not to sit with my mom, and my shame of her mingled with my own guilt. I don't recall that she ever came after me and insisted that I sit with the family. In fact, it was never mentioned, as if my absence was not even noticed. Or maybe Mom realized she needed to let me make my own choices.

As I sat isolated from my mother, I felt the disconnect. I knew this was not how it was supposed to be, but I had to separate myself from my shabby-looking mother. The worst part of this experience was that I felt really bad about myself because I believed that what I was doing was wrong, and I did it anyway.

Years later, it occurred to me that choosing to sit apart from my mother and my sisters—our dad had long since stopped going to church—was my first experience at asserting myself and going against what I perceived to be the expectation of others. When I wasn't absorbed in the guilt, I somehow felt empowered by doing what I wanted without being afraid of displeasing. But oh, what a price I paid.

Chapter Fifteen

THE EVER-PRESENT
THREAT OF VIOLENCE

I never grew accustomed to living with someone dangerous, someone I could not escape. Our prison walls were not made of steel or wire. They were the bonds that exist between a child and parent and siblings, those invisible boundaries that are meant to keep a family together, counting on each other, dependent on parents for safety and well-being. The ever-present threat of violence and the bond I felt with my father created an inner conflict that far exceeded my understanding or the skills needed to talk about it, much less resolve it.

It wasn't just the acts of violence, the physical attacks and verbal lashings my dad heaped on my mother. It was the realization that we were living with someone who was dangerous, someone we could not escape. Although I lived with terror day after day, I never became accustomed to the fear that permeated every fiber of my being. Even when I was supposed to be playing and having fun, fear hovered over me like a black cloud that periodically swooped down and enveloped me from the inside out. There was no escape from this threat.

As the firstborn, my bonds with my father were strong. I remembered the pre-terror times when he played with me and taught me to cover my mouth when I sneezed or coughed and how to tie my shoestrings. I even remember him taking me aside once when we were in a crowd of people we didn't know. He stooped down to my four-year old level and talked with me about being careful around strangers. I can't recall his actual words, but the message has never left me.

I remember that as a small child, I wanted to be with him. I followed him around and watched whatever he was doing. I just wanted to be there. When he was working on his car, I wanted to help. He would send me to get a tool or some other item, and I felt really grown up when I could help. But then he would scold me when I returned with the wrong item.

One time my father took me with him when he went hunting for squirrels. Since he rarely took anyone along, I felt so special walking along beside him in the woods. But this feeling faded when he scolded me for making too much noise when the dead leaves crunched beneath my feet. He knew how to walk without making a sound. I did not have that skill.

His criticism of me increased as his abuse of Mom escalated. I could do nothing right, no matter how hard I tried. And I did try. At first, I wanted to please him because he was my dad. In time, I tried to please him because I was afraid of him and wanted to avoid the assault of his displeasure. My failure to meet his demand fast enough or perfect enough always resulted in a verbal lashing or possibly a slap or shove, all of which frightened me. I wanted to be with my father, but I also didn't. At times, I went to great lengths to avoid him. I concluded that there must be something wrong with me.

There were times when he would be nice to me, that is, he was less demanding. But this did not last. My anger toward him grew and deepened, but I dared not express it. I think the possibility of responding to him in anger was blocked by my fear of him. So the anger lodged deep within my heart where I also felt love for him. This was confusing. I could not put all of this together. I loved my dad; he loved me. But he was mean, and I was deathly afraid of him.

If you asked me what I dreaded most—my dad's deadening silence, his violent outbursts, or the chaos that followed—I could not answer. He always scared me. Sometimes I wonder why I never ran away, why it never occurred to me to try to leave this place where I never felt safe.

When I think of our home, I remember that I was so sure that there was no other home like this one. There could be no other home where you could never count on things being the same from one hour to the next. I never knew how my dad was going to be, what he would do, or what he would demand of us. It was his mood, after all, that determined how we would be or what we would do. I would measure my day by how he felt, what he needed or commanded.

His sullen moodiness could blacken even the sunniest of days. Waiting for his next command was a unique form of imprisonment that any onlooker would have never suspected. His cold intimidation and my internalization of fear weaved its tentacles throughout my being. I could never escape. I had seen the bruises my mother bore when she once dared to resist his force. The feel of his leather belt against my legs remained fresh in my memory, administered because I had not moved fast enough to do his bidding. I wore the bruises for a week, hopeful that none of my classmates would ask me about them. No one ever did.

Weekends were the worst, especially if Dad stayed home. I, of course, preferred that he leave. When he was not there, I could breathe. My sisters and I could play without having to be quiet. On rare occasions during the many evenings he spent at the tavern, Mom would play her guitar and tell us stories about when she was a kid. But even as I listened to her stories, I felt the heavy dread of how it would be when he came home.

That feeling never left me. I carried it constantly, even when I was doing something I liked doing. Life at home was always spoiled by what was happening or what was about to happen. The chaos never ceased. It was always going on inside of me, whether he was present or not. Because there was no predictability to our days or evenings, I learned to always be on the alert and ready, although I had no idea of what I would do when something happened.

Even though I was less than six years old when my father's abuse began, there were things I did know, things no one ever told me. I knew Mom did not want to talk about my dad's violence. I think she thought we didn't know what was going on, but I did. I knew she worried a lot about his drinking and about the money we didn't have for food and school. I knew I should never talk about how it was in our home. I knew that my two little sisters were scared, and there were times when I had to get them away from our dad when he was treating Mom badly. I knew I had to find some way to distract them. I figured out what to do as I went along, and I guess it helped. Maybe it helped me the most. I needed to not see or hear what was scaring me. I knew I couldn't cry because that would scare my little sisters even more. I knew how to pretend that everything was all right, even when it wasn't.

My favorite thing to do, when I could, was to be alone, away from the things that scared me. The woods that stretched for miles on the backside of our property were my haven. Chores and homework done, I would run down the path that led to the trees that stood with open arms and welcomed me. The branches of my favorite tree dipped in the wind, as if to scoop me up, and if it was low enough, I could crawl carefully up and pretend to be far away from everyone. Her rough barky skin was like a caress to my own. I would lean against her trunk and feel so at home. When I was not in or under a tree, I played in the little creek that wandered nearby. The water gurgling around my toes was a touch

I enjoyed. I imagined I heard the little creek telling me all about where she had come from, and sometimes I tried to follow along to see where she was going. I could always count on the trees and the creek to be there, and I always felt safe when I was with them. But then I had to leave and go back home, where the only thing I could count on was chaos and violence.

There were no written or spoken rules in my home. Even so, I lived in constant fear of breaking the one rule that had been communicated so fiercely that its grip strangled any possible expression of spontaneity. I'm not sure at what point I got it—that nothing must ever be done or said that would upset my father. By age six, I had learned the consequences of violating this boundary. I was terrified by what he would do and say when something displeased him. I struggled to understand what it was that set off his rage, but it kept changing, depending on what—I never knew. With all my might, I tried to please him, though it required me to give up any thought of what I wanted. This was how we all survived, especially Mom. This unspoken priority dominated every moment of our existence as a family and held me in bondage to a person who terrified me, someone I both loved and hated.

Bound to a father who showed no interest in me, I was never free from fear. In the classroom, I alternated between being preoccupied with what might happen that night and wanting to answer the teacher's question. The voice in my head asserted what I had come to believe about myself. "I'm probably wrong. What if I can't say it right?" I knew everyone would laugh at me. So instead of raising my hand, I sank deeper into the hard wooden seat and listened while someone else gave my answer.

Though I could not name the feeling that welled up inside of me as I sat in silence, it did not feel good. A sense of failure that translated in the years to follow as "not good enough" eventually soaked into everything I did and became an identity I carried well into my thirties. There were so many missed opportunities, and I never experienced someone saying to me, "Well done, Helen."

One of the ways I escaped the pain of my felt failure was to lose myself in reading. Books, other than those I brought home from school, were a rarity in our household, except for one, the family album. It had been carefully compiled and preserved by my mom who had taken most of the pictures herself with an old Brownie camera. My favorite indoor pastime was leafing through it, wondering who it was that peopled those pages. I always noticed that there were very few pictures of my father and even fewer pictures of him with us.

One photo of all of us was deeply etched into my memory. It was taken on a sunny day in May of 1948, my First Holy Communion day. My dad was dressed in a suit, the only time I remember seeing him wear it. He was standing near Mom, next to the old Lilac bush, flanked by my sisters and me, dressed in my white dress and veil. He smiled and held a bottle of whiskey, its label facing the camera, his pride having nothing to do with me.

I remember the precise moment when I understood how little interest he had in what was, for me, a momentous occasion. I had anticipated and carefully prepared for this day, the first special day of my young life of seven years. Any feelings of joy I had were overshadowed by the short-lived celebration of this new stage of my life. It all ended once the camera captured that moment, so as not to let me forget what happened next. The picture taken, my father turned and walked away to go drinking with his brother. It was all over as far as he was concerned.

The aura of the festivities, such as they were, faded as I watched him walk away without a word. I ran into the house, up to our attic room, and removed my white dress and veil. I laid aside these ritual garments designed to be worn on this day only. The tears that welled up inside me seemed to fill the vast emptiness left by my father's departure.

Did he have any idea of what had taken place that day? Did he care? Did he ever think about his children, about me, his oldest? I wonder if he ever had any hopes or dreams for me, any thoughts about who I would become or what I would do with my life. I wonder if it really mattered to him. I really would like to know. I will never know.

Chapter Sixteen

LEARNED ABANDONMENT

To survive my father's abuse, mom let go of her own needs, preferences, and feelings. She hid her feelings (hurt, fear) from us. Cut off from her own feelings, she had not only abandoned herself, she had also become emotionally unavailable to us. To protect herself, she had to sever emotional ties with her children. Thus, she modeled self-abandonment as a way to cope. As a child, my sense of self evolved in emotional isolation where I learned to disregard and disown myself. In my adult life, I discovered that my real self was nowhere to be found.

My memories of Mom are so mixed. I enjoy recalling the preschool days when our dad was off being a soldier in the Army, and Mom was busy being our mom. Sometime she worked in the fields and helped Uncle Jimmy, her brother, with the crops. This is where she first began to know my dad when he worked as a field hand.

When she was home from the fields and doing house chores, we could come running into the house anytime with a new discovery or a skinned knee. She listened intently and took care of us. Often she was fully focused on my sister and me. She made our clothes, played house with us, played her guitar, and sang to us. At the end of a long day, she would rub our tired little legs and tuck us in with a night prayer. We missed our dad, so we would pray for him. He had sent me a picture of himself, which I kept under my pillow.

Following his return several years later, tensions grew and Mom's attentive time with us all but disappeared. She always seemed preoccupied. I started first grade at age five. Our little sister was born the next year, and by now his drinking and abusive behavior had increased. Mom had little time for us, even as we were being terrorized, because it was all she could do to cope with his verbal, emotional, and physical attacks.

As a result of the abuse, she ignored her own needs as a way of coping. It also drew her away from us, drained her of energy, and distracted her from her emotional responsibility to us, her children.

The distance between our hearts stretched beyond our capacity to reach each other—she, the victim; me, her eldest daughter, who was emotionally disconnected from her, yet felt very responsible for two little sisters who needed more than I could give them. But I learned quickly to shift from being focused on my fear to protecting my little sisters from their fear. I learned at this very early age to set aside my own feelings and try to help them be less afraid. Here were the roots of my becoming the "family hero," the "rescuer," the one with no needs, strong like Mom.

When I think of Mom, I think of the price she paid to keep our family together and how she modeled life for us. She seldom told us what to do or not do. She was too busy surviving. But I learned so much from her. Never complain; never gossip; work hard and sacrifice; be considerate and generous; grow plants; be determined, never give up; always do your best.

And there were other lessons I learned when I had no voice—lessons in self-abandonment. What you want or need isn't important; always put the other person's needs first; the man is in charge and gets whatever he wants, no matter what; hide your feelings; never talk about what bothers you; keep giving the other a chance to change, even if he hurts you.

As Mom abandoned herself, she put her feelings in a place where I could not feel them. I had no access to what she experienced because she had blocked it from herself, as well as from us. She could not express her true self; she was emotionally absent. I knew she loved me, though I never felt her love. I learned well this way of being strong that she so effectively modeled.

I did not know I was learning lessons in self-abandonment. What child does? We simply go along and absorb life in the beginning. Right? We know the adults are in charge, especially Mom and Dad. We count on them for everything: food, clothing, shelter, love, safety, and protection from harm. We trust them instinctively. We belong to them and cling to them, even when any one or more of these things are not provided. Even if it hurts.

Physical presence is no safeguard against emotional abandonment. Mom was always there. When I close my eyes, I can see her on cold wintery mornings, up before dawn making a fire in the old wood stove so that it would be warm for us when we got up. I see her in the kitchen preparing meals, out hanging the wash on the clothesline, working in the garden, milking the cow, mending our clothes, cleaning the house. I remember that I missed her when she eventually went to work at the local doll factory, and I would run to meet her at the end of the day.

As a child, I don't remember being held by her or being complimented when I did something that pleased her. I don't remember ever feeling recognized or special to her. Nor do I recall any kind of interaction with Mom that would even hint of a conversation. As a matter of fact, I seldom spoke to this person who felt so distant, so inaccessible. I was convinced that what I thought and felt was not important to her, that I was not important to her. And so, my thoughts and fears and worries and periodic joys never left the shelter of my heart.

An introvert by nature, I lived in my shyness and felt very bad about who I was, very insecure and always afraid that others would discover my badness. Because no one ever told me that I was good, I was sure there was something wrong with me. I was filled with anxiety about being found out. Keeping my mouth shut became my safety net, while inside I was continually processing my observations, what I would do or not do, what I thought the other person was thinking of me. My thoughts swirled in an endless loop of processing the past and the future; guessing and anticipating. I had no voice and little time for play and laughter.

As little children, we are basically at the mercy of the adults in our lives because we are in a world we have yet to learn. We still need to develop concepts, understanding, and words with which to express our concerns and feelings. We may feel fear but have little means of talking about what scares us. If what scares us is our own father's words and actions, how do we process such an experience that feels so wrong? This man is my dad, my protector, but he hurts my mom, the one who takes care of me. As little ones, we lack the skills, the words, and the voice with which to talk about our fears. And if we did, who would listen?

Commentary on the experience of emotional abandonment

We have much to learn about emotional abandonment: what it is, how it happens, how we learn it, and its long-term consequences. First, it should be noted that this is a condition that is not limited to children who experience family violence. Many dysfunctional situations can contribute to this, including but not limited to:

- Adults who are emotionally ill-equipped to parent
- Parents who are occupied with their own struggles in their relationship
- Parents who fail to communicate with their children, verbally or emotionally

- Children who are left to fend for themselves and are emotionally alone in the midst of struggles, with no guidance or reassurance

Emotional abandonment, as it is being considered here, is about a child being left without support (disconnected) at the emotional level at a time when feeling loved, valued, and wanted is critical to how she feels about herself, how she perceives the world, and how she begins to define who she is within the world. Without feedback that helps her feel good about herself, she is likely to experience the disintegration of her thoughts, feelings, and behavior. These three functions usually follow each other and reflect an integrated wholeness within the personality. When thoughts, feelings, and behaviors are not integrated, they each move in different directions and sometimes operate separately, causing a disparity between the outer person and the inner self.

Thinking

For example, I was always *thinking*, interpreting what was happening, and figuring out what to do and how to survive. I thought in isolation, without the benefit of any mature input or guidance, always from a perspective of fear and uncertainty. I had no context, other than my own, in which to formulate my thoughts. I even projected what I thought others were thinking about me, "knowing" that they saw me as "bad." I believed that to be true, and I put more weight on what I imagined their thoughts to be, instead of trusting my own. Despite my distorted thinking, I wanted to present myself as "perfect."

Feeling

I denied my *feelings*, though not consciously. My anger was masked by obedience, submissiveness, and perfectionism. I never expressed my fear, which allowed me to ignore it. Living with unaddressed fear ensured that I would not feel joy, something I knew I didn't deserve. In order to please others and avoid their possible anger, I dismissed my own desires. I didn't mention my needs or concerns for fear of adding to Mom's burden. Feelings of shame and guilt were buried.

Behavior

My *behavior* mirrored what I thought others expected of me and did not reflect my true thoughts or feelings. I screened everything before I spoke or acted, and what I did was often contrary to what I actually wanted to do. My behavior was guided more by what I felt others thought of me than what was true for me. Beneath all of this was a deep fear of rejection—a rejection of the person I perceived as totally undesirable, unlikable—the self I wanted to be as invisible as possible. This disintegration remained with me into adulthood and created multiple problems.

Commentary on "learned" emotional abandonment

With no intent to demonize either of my parents or anyone else's, I want to focus on and identify what is involved in the process of learning to abandon oneself emotionally.

We've all been children. We all learned how to walk and talk and dress ourselves. We all survived the developmental stages from baby, to toddler, to being a kid, a teenager, and then beyond. Depending on our personality, we either emerged as little persons who could easily express ourselves, or we tended to be less expressive. No matter which, we all carried a multitude of feelings that we learned how to express—or not. Indeed, childhood is a vital time of learning, and our parents taught us some of what we learned through direct intervention, but much of it was simply absorbed. Remember?

I do remember. As a small child, I felt everything. I was always trying to sense what was happening so that I knew what to do next.

I was always attuned to the potential for danger, perhaps because of my volatile environment. My hyper-vigilance was usually accompanied by feelings of fear, anxiety, helplessness, confusion, and sadness. I did not yet have words for these feelings; I was too young. Only today do I have the words to describe that experience: I was vulnerable and very alone.

Mom was the only one I could count on. My father was not safe. I feared his gruffness, his verbal threats, his moodiness and his drunkenness, his angry outbursts, and the way he treated Mom. I feared that at any time she could be taken from our lives.

I watched my mother very carefully. She seemed far away. I could not feel her, and I never knew what she was feeling. She seldom spoke, and when she did, it was never about what was happening to her.

She was preoccupied with survival while trying to take care of our basic needs, but I didn't know that then. She never knew what I really needed. She had numbed herself, had blocked her feelings as a way of coping with the abuse. This required her to abandon not only her own feelings, but her needs, dreams, and support system. She became emotionally unavailable to us, her children.

Because she was out of touch with her own feelings, needs, and longings, she was alienated from her real self. She could not be herself. She had to appear strong, to show no emotion, and she could never cry in our presence, even in the face of brutality. Perhaps she thought she was protecting us. In reality, she had abandoned herself and us. It was an emotional abandonment. This is what she modeled as a way to cope with life's difficulties.

I not only felt that Mom was unavailable, I learned to block any awareness of my own feelings that I could not tolerate, and I became unavailable to myself. Mom did this in order to survive and to keep the family together. I did it in order to help Mom. I had to be strong for my little sisters and do whatever I could at home to ease her burden. I would not cry, would never talk about my debilitating fears, could never identify my anger as anger toward my parents, could never be myself. At a very early age, I abandoned what was real about me and became an empty shell that I did not like.

I did not have my mom's emotional support during my years of cognitive development, so I evolved with a very poor sense of self. I was obsessed with thoughts about what had happened or what was going to happen and tried to figure out how I would respond, always feeling so insecure and fearful of making a mistake. I always believed that I would.

To protect the self that I perceived as inadequate and unacceptable, I created ways to respond to protect myself from further hurt or rejection. These defenses were my way to survive. They included: not needing or wanting anything, being extremely good and obedient, remaining silent and invisible, people-pleasing, and minimizing and disowning my feelings.

These responses that became my patterns of thinking/feeling/behaving are the consequences of learned emotional abandonment that I address in more detail in the next chapter.

Significant damage occurs when a child, in the presence of threatening events, has to interpret for herself what is happening and figure out how to respond without having any emotional support or guidance. To arrive at adulthood and discover that one's real self is nowhere in sight is one of the most devastating consequences.

Chapter Seventeen

PATTERNS OF
HIDDEN THOUGHTS,
BURIED FEELINGS,
REVEALING BEHAVIORS

*"By naming the inner patterns that imprison us,
we come to know them more fully and obtain
a certain power over them."*

—Sue Monk Kidd

When I was four years old, my mother made a dress for me that I can still see when I close my eyes. It was white with blue stripes from top to bottom with no belt, a Peter Pan collar, and a pocket that depicted a little birdhouse. She had sewn a few bright blue birds near the birdhouse pocket. I remember watching Mom draw pictures on white paper and then cut different pieces of colored fabric to match the shapes, which she then sewed on to my dress. She, herself, had designed the pattern that guided her to make this creation.

I have often thought that the patterns of *learned self-abandonment* and other strategies for survival are similar, in that they can guide a process, a way of responding to life. It is different, however, because it is something we construct within our self that eventually becomes an established, habitual way of thinking, feeling, and behaving. While these patterns provide a familiar and comfortable way of interacting with life, they also confine us and limit us from other possibilities.

These are structured patterns of response that operate at the unconscious level but become an integral part of who we perceive ourselves to be, often distorting and covering up who we really are. They are a collection of thoughts, feelings, and behaviors that are based on certain assumptions about ourselves and how we are to relate to the world. We are often unaware of these assumptions/beliefs, so we rarely examine or question them. These beliefs determine the inner patterns we create for ourselves, and they become our strategies for survival. They become integral to our identity. Who would we be without them? These life patterns run deep, similar to the roots of the elm tree that shaded my grandmother's home, and like those embedded and winding tendrils, they aren't easily extracted.

I have no doubt about how strong and deeply rooted my own patterns are, patterns I created as a child who needed to survive the terror of my father's violence. I have spent much of my life becoming aware of these survival strategies, and have learned to identify which ones still influence my choices, dismantling some and modifying others. Because I did survive, many of these patterns of thought, feeling, and behavior have been like cherished toys I did not plan to discard. Nevermind that some were only ghosts of who I really am. Nevermind that most of the patterns were based on false beliefs that I did not consciously understand. That is, until I encountered a traumatic disruption in my adult life and found myself face-to-face with thoughts, emotions, and behaviors that were not appropriate for a thirty-something in that situation. These experiences caused me to wake up to my inner world and resulted in deep soul-searching. They became more frequent in my forties and fifties, and were usually related to some form of loss and grief.

During these painful times, I was stopped in my tracks and had the choice to either go mad or to look at my history and face the consequences. I chose the latter. Partly by trial and error, partly with the help of psychotherapy, and always with the support of loved ones in my life, I faced the ghosts—ghosts that presented a false image that I believed was actually me. I learned a lot about myself and the patterns in which I was deeply invested, as well as their underlying assumptions.

There are specific cognitive/emotional/behavioral patterns that, like my mother when she designed my dress, I used to define my life. Some of these may have been based on a long-standing script passed on from previous generations of my parents' families. Mom grew up on a farm where she and her four siblings had responsibilities at a very early age. Their father, in addition to being a farmer, was also a shepherd and a man of reflection. Their mom was of Irish and English descent and had a great sense of humor. I remember them as a harmonious family, enjoyable to be with. My father, on the other hand, grew up in a family with six siblings who saw their father abuse their mom. Grandpa alternated his work as a tiff miner with regular bouts of drunkenness and frequent absence from the home. Grandma was a serious, deeply religious woman. Both were of French and German descent. There were very weak bonds among the family members, many of whom were not easy to be with.

I now understand the strengths and weaknesses of each of these families and the influence they exerted on me. As the family script was passed on to me, it provided some of the initial tools I used to craft my early patterns of response to life within my family.

As a small child, I knew that my living environment was not safe. I was terrified and ill-prepared to cope with my unrelenting fear. I had to develop ways to survive, so I blended our family script with various survival strategies, and thus created my own inner program of conditioned responses that became my patterns of perceiving, thinking, feeling, and behaving. Early on, I learned that being a good girl—obedient, silent, and responsible—was rewarded. It kept me out of harm's way. These methods of staying safe generated a multitude of other patterns that I identify and discuss in this chapter. They initially helped me survive the family violence, but later became problematic.

I was in my late thirties before I understood that I was creating some of my own problems by the way I looked at and thought about myself and my life. The responses that had once worked for me, and indeed helped me, no longer worked. My ways of coping used to help me feel a little more secure, but now they didn't fit the person I was becoming. Hyper-responsibility, perfectionism, and the fear of being discovered were all patterns that conflicted with what life required of me as a mature adult. In time, and with growing insight into the dissonance I felt, my inner emotional and psychological structures began to disintegrate and left me deeply depressed and dysfunctional. This dark period was exceptionally painful because my very identity was threatened. If I acknowledged my vulnerability and allowed myself to be seen, who would I be? How would I survive? It was time for me to face the ghosts and to learn what held me in its grasp.

What I remember most about this dark part of my journey was the loneliness of standing stripped of the so-called security I had tried so hard to preserve through my teen and young adult years. In this torturous place where I was conquering the ghosts, to my bewilderment I met the angry, hurt, and frightened child who cowered within me. She resisted with all her might my efforts to look at her, to embrace her, and eventually, to get to know her. After all, I had abandoned her a long time ago.

That part of my story must wait for now. In the meantime, I will tell you what I learned about the patterns I developed, eventually identified, and began to dismantle as I gradually got to know and lovingly accept the inner me I had once forsaken. They reflect the ways in which I learned to abandon myself. Some still emerge in varying degrees, as healing is an on-going process. Like the repetition of the seasons, each cycle reveals something not previously seen.

The patterns I developed

At age five, I was terrified of my father's behavior and what he was doing to my mom. I had nothing but my own feelings to guide me, and I was afraid most of the time. During this very formative period of my development, I began to figure out ways to survive, and by age six, I learned how to protect my sisters.

The basic ingredients necessary for developing healthy relationships—a major function of the family—are trust, emotional bonds, and feeling safe. These were absent in my home. In fact, the patterns I developed to survive were based on assumptions that were completely contrary to these necessities.

An assumption, according to Webster, is "a fact or statement taken for granted." As a small child, I *thought* about what happened in my family, but the truth is, I mostly *felt* my experience. I sensed my mom's struggle. I sensed danger. I sensed my little sisters' fear and need for comfort. I absorbed the violent energy that passed between my parents. These were realities that I assumed were true.

I also assumed that my mom and dad knew everything, or at least more than I did. I assumed that whatever they presented to me, verbally or physically, must be true. One of these truths was that there was something wrong with me. They never really talked with me or communicated anything different. My dad repeatedly told me that I couldn't do anything right, and Mom never denied it. In fact, she expressed little interest in me or my life.

I already knew that I was bad because I didn't do anything to protect my mom when my dad hurt her. I felt bad all the time, which proved all that I believed about myself. These assumptions framed my beliefs about myself, my world, and how I was to relate to it.

Based upon these assumed—but false—truths, I unconsciously developed patterns that guided the next years of my life. My conditioned responses to people and situations, that defined my experiences and trapped me in repetitive and destructive ways of thinking, feeling, and behaving, are described below.

Poor sense of self

Little children sense that they are safe and lovable by how they are treated. Parents communicate acceptance and love when they hold their child, look into her eyes and smile when they talk to her, and attend to her needs while they gently but firmly set boundaries. From the very beginning, the child needs to feel loved, wanted, and safe. Throughout her development, parents and others need to reflect back to the child that she is good and worthy of their love and attention. If she does something unacceptable, they help her understand that her behavior was rejected, not her. All of this will help her feel good about herself. She can then begin to develop a strong and positive sense of who she is.

I did not have this foundation, and I remember an all-consuming feeling that I was bad. I knew that I was different from the other children. Play was difficult. They seemed to have fun, but I could not. I worried about Mom. When I chose not to go to the playground with the other kids, I felt even worse because I knew I should have been there. I knew I was inferior to the others and had nothing to offer. And even if I did, I would never do it as well as anyone else. I was filled with shame, and that feeling of wrong-being and worthlessness was rooted in my internal isolation. No one reflected anything different back to me, so I hid the self I didn't like, the self I was sure no one else could like.

Invisibility

Even though I excelled at school, was obedient, and pleased the adults in my life, none of these external behaviors relieved my feelings about the awful person I thought I was. I didn't want anyone to find out how bad I really was, so I developed ways of not being seen or heard. I seldom talked or spoke up when I had a question or had something to say. Rather than speak up, I pretended that everything was okay in certain situations. I withheld information. If I wanted or needed something, I would not ask for it for a variety of reasons, including the fear of rejection. I did not want to be seen or found out. I was gripped by fear that this bad, shameful, inferior, and worthless person would be seen, found out, and rejected. Being on the playground was too painful to endure, and I knew that any interaction with the other children would reveal the bad person that I was. I could not walk into a room full of people without great anxiety, and I avoided doing so whenever I could.

People-pleasing

I wanted so much to be liked, to be seen as good—though I knew better—and to be accepted. I learned to anticipate what was needed and made every effort to provide it. I did chores at home partly to help Mom and partly because it was a way I could please her. I only said what I thought the other person wanted to hear; I did what I thought they wanted done, which often required me to minimize or even deny what I needed or wanted. I was compliant when I didn't want to be. I always deferred to the other as a means of pleasing them. There is so much that I never expressed, out of fear that I would displease someone. I lived from the outside in.

Perfectionism

I was deathly afraid to make a mistake or that I would not do something well enough. This fear was nurtured by my father who frequently told me that I could never do anything right. Whenever I fetched the tool he wanted, I knew I would bring back the wrong one. I trembled with fear all the way to the toolbox and all the way back. He heaped his venom upon me and screamed at me for my mistake, and I wondered why he bothered to ask for my help. I strove to be perfect in every area of my life, though of course, it was never really to my satisfaction. Being perfect was a way of seeking acceptance based on my performance. The fear of not being able to do something perfectly often blocked me from expressing myself, which was another form of self-abandonment.

Need for order

Even though our house was quite dilapidated, at age six I picked things up off the floor, made the beds, cleaned the ashtrays, and kept order in the room I shared with my sisters. When I created order, I felt protected from the discomfort caused by the violence and chaotic unpredictability in our home. It also gave me a sense of being in control when so much of our life seemed out of control. Certainly, my dad was often out of control.

Need to control

The need to control is a very strong force that manifested itself, not only in regard to controlling my environment, but also in trying to manipulate people, situations, and their outcomes. One of the ways I used this strategy was to withhold information. In certain situations, I thought I could keep someone from becoming angry with me if I didn't tell the whole story or if I left out the part that might upset them or cause them to think less of me. But it didn't stop there. My attempts to control another person would often morph into accepting responsibilities that were not mine, especially when I wanted to fix the situation or control the outcome.

Heightened Sense of Responsibility

Being overly responsible gave me the illusion of being in control, and it also covered up painful feelings. Being responsible gave me a reason to feel better about myself. I could look at all the good that I was doing and think, *maybe I am worthwhile after all.* This fed my belief that my value came from outside myself, and it also led me to ignore important boundaries, to take responsibility for what was not mine to mind, and to neglect my own needs—yet another expression of self-abandonment. Eventually, I saw that this pattern gave me permission to avoid my own issues. Being overly responsible for other people and situations was a way to shirk my responsibility to myself, a self that did not deserve my love and attention. This pattern thrived on my denying or at least minimizing what I felt, needed, and wanted.

Minimizing needs, wants, feelings

Of all the patterns, I believe this one is the most self-defeating, and it operated below my awareness. I seldom recognized that I minimized myself. When, out of my need to please, I deferred to what the other person wanted, I rarely noticed the underlying feeling of anxiety. Or, if I wanted to go to a specific place but the other person preferred an alternative, I never felt that what I wanted was as important as what they wanted, and therefore I never asserted my preference. As for my own needs, I denied them. If I felt a need, I simply ignored it. I knew I didn't deserve anything beyond what I got. This was my way to disconnect from my feelings, another form of self-abandonment.

Boundary Confusion

When there is no strong sense of self, it is impossible to know where you end and the other person begins. It is difficult to know where your feelings and opinions start and stop and where the other's begins. That invisible boundary that separates each of us as a unique and valuable person—so necessary for healthy relating—cannot develop and thrive when we do not know that we are loved and valued. Boundaries emerge from a belief about what we deserve or don't deserve. It is in the family context where we, as little children, begin to learn where the boundaries are and how to set them at the physical, emotional, and intellectual levels.

I had great difficulty in this area of my life, both as a child and in later years, not only because boundary-setting was not modeled for me, but also because I did not like or respect myself. In addition, my all-absorbing fear would not allow me to set limits because I would have to assert myself and risk rejection. This fostered a pattern of boundary confusion that, at times, made me unable to separate myself from a problem, from work, or from a person.

Hyper-vigilance

This is a common pattern for someone who has experienced various forms of trauma. When my father was present, at home or anticipated, I was always on the alert, watching and listening for clues about what might happen next. I had to pick up on what he was feeling, learn his moods, and anticipate his next act. I always expected the worst and felt a need to be prepared—but prepared for what? Minor incidents in our home quickly become major conflicts between our mom and dad. Even if he barely raised his voice, I cringed, my body tightened, and I would be on full alert to run from the room or house at any moment. When I waited for him to come home from work, I was like a sentry who anticipated the enemy.

Though this pattern has diminished in my life, I still don't think my body knows it. Even at rest, I sometimes find that I'm holding myself in a taut position.

Avoidance of Conflict

While most people I've met don't like conflict, children who grew up in a violent home will usually, as adults, do anything to avoid conflict even if what they do or don't do proves detrimental to themselves. As a child, I withheld information from my parents in order to avoid triggering an argument, even if it was something I needed to tell them. After I left home, I avoided my father altogether because we could not get along. He thought his way was the only way, but I knew better. During my young adult life, in order to avoid conflict, I didn't do things I wanted to do. Rooted in fear, as so many of these patterns are, this one continues to haunt me at times.

Take life and self too serious

I acknowledge, but choose not to dwell on, the fact that my father's terrorizing behavior created a living environment that made it difficult to be a child. As in so many other dysfunctional situations, we had to grow up fast. There was no time to be a carefree child. Life was very serious, and we lived with the daily threat of being destroyed. I was never free of that fear, even when at play. I was preoccupied with surviving both the terror of my home and the feelings it generated, feelings I could not tolerate. I closed those feelings off, which caused great collateral damage because I also closed off other feelings, like the feeling of joy. The spontaneity that comes with play and using the imagination was squelched by the tendency to take myself and life very serious. I saw only the shading, the dark side, the anticipation of the worst, the stuff to worry about, and the loss. The child in me was forsaken at an early age. The tendrils of this pattern still hold me in their grip.

Closing

Emotional abandonment is, indeed, the mother of many problematic cognitive, emotional, and behavioral patterns. It would be years before I recognized, with the help of a therapist, that I had learned to abandon myself through the strategies I had developed—a concept that I have only in recent years come to understand.

While these patterns/strategies helped me to survive and allowed me to interact with the daily threats I could not escape, they also caused me to define myself in a distorted way that ignored my strengths. In order to redefine who I was, I had to let go of those distortions and embrace, with love and compassion, the self that I had learned to abandon. The paradox of this strange process bears highlighting: I was emotionally abandoned by my mother, so I felt worthless and worked hard to hide my shameful self. Because I feared further abandonment, I developed strategies and patterns to survive, and through them, effectively abandoned myself.

How would I find the part of me I had abandoned? How could I reclaim the self I had disowned? What was I to do with these deep-rooted patterns that had guided my thoughts, feelings, and behavior for so many years? These were not easy questions to face in my forties and fifties. The journey out of family violence began with struggling but has now become one of "living into the answer," as the poet Rilke advises. It was a slow, humbling process to discover and then claim my strengths that emerged as the old patterns that were buried in my subconscious were transformed. I had to break free from the prison of those patterns that held me hostage and didn't allow me to see and embrace the truth of who I really am.

The process to reclaim my abandoned self was a long journey through darkness into discovery.

PART IV

EMBRACING THE ABANDONED SELF

Chapter Eighteen

THROUGH DARKNESS
TO DISCOVERY

Now you must go out into your heart as onto a vast plain.
Now the immense loneliness begins.

—Rainer M. Rilke

I cringe when I remember my teen years, characterized by my internal isolation that left me feeling disconnected from the outside world. Since childhood, I knew that I was a bad person. I had failed to protect my mom. I had never done anything good enough to win my father's approval. I pretended everything was all right when it wasn't. I saw myself as repugnant to my peers. I was so afraid others would see my defectiveness.

I left home in September of 1958, with my sixteen-year-old mind focused on one thing: find a job and help Mom pay off some of the bills, a heavy burden that she carried. In the end, it was a way for me to start over where no one knew me. It was also my way out of the unbearable environment at home. I got a job washing pots and pans in the cafeteria at St. Mary's Hospital in St. Louis, and during my off hours, I studied to complete my senior year of high school through correspondence courses. With no social skills or friends, I was painfully aware of what I perceived as personal limitations. My social ineptness was more evidence that there was something wrong with me. I was this bad person no one wanted to be with. I concluded that the only way I could save my soul was to dedicate my life to God by joining a religious community. After researching several other groups, I applied to and was accepted by the Sisters of St. Mary with whom I worked.

On a sultry August 9th in 1959, I said goodbye to my family and exchanged my lay clothes for the long, black habit. When I look at pictures taken that day, I am struck by the sadness I see in the faces of my parents. This was such an unexpressed emotion in our family. I had no idea that my departure would have that effect on them. Nor did I realize that I would carry into my new life all the guilt of having failed my mother, the fear of my father, my distorted sense of self, as well as my need to remain invisible, to please, to be perfect, to be overly responsible. These latter characteristics allowed me to adapt with ease to the convent structure that required obedience to superiors, personal perfection, less concern for one's own needs, always with a focus on the needs of others. It was easy to remain hidden in an environment that did not encourage self-expression, especially if it varied from the norm.

As Sister Gabriella, I immersed myself into my new family where there was predictability and a sense of security I had never known. I loved the women with whom I shared my new life and appreciated the opportunities and challenges that shaped me in the years that followed. Still, I continued to struggle inwardly with the feeling that I was always on the outside looking in, never meeting expectations, never good enough. I was thirty-seven when I journaled:

> *Often my motivation, my decisions are based upon reality outside myself. What does the other person think or expect of me? Rarely do I do something because I want to do it. Living from the outside in, coupled with defensiveness, need for approval, and fear of conflict is a painful way to live.*

I wrote this entry at a time when I lived peacefully with a small community of four other nuns in a house a few blocks from our Congregational Convent. Even when all seemed to go well in my life, the sense that there was something wrong with me shadowed me like a black cloud. In my quiet moments of reflection, I was keenly aware of my discontent.

One quiet Sunday afternoon in 1979, I went to my room on the second floor to read and reflect. The September sun played through the branches of the maple tree outside my window and created puddles of light on my pale green bedspread. The hall clock downstairs chimed three o'clock. I leaned back in my rocker and closed my eyes. I thought of Mom, a widow of only a few months since my father died from the effects of cancer and alcoholism. I cried a little when he died, mostly for Mom. She never talked about his death, so I don't know if she felt the same relief I felt. He was gone. At last, the giant boulder I had carried all these years slipped off my shoulders and vanished.

In the midst of these quiet ruminations, a door deep within my consciousness burst open. Images rushed out, long ago memories flooded my awareness with a shocking force. All the energy I had previously used to block these memories now pushed me into a dark space. Scenes of my father attacking my mother were played out in front of me. His violence flashed through me, jarring me with all the terror I felt as a six-year-old when I watched my mom collapse under the blow of his fist. The weight of his large body held her down as he continued to beat her. She tried to protect her head. She cried out. Eventually, there was silence.

I was afraid he would kill her. I gathered my little sisters and ran out to the woodshed, away from this unbearable scene. We didn't talk. I tried to think of some way to distract them. I thought a walk in the woods would help, but it was too dark. I was never sure when to return to the house, never knew when it would be safe.

Alone in my room that sunny day, I watched as other scenes flashed by. I saw my father slap Mom, drag her across the floor, and curse her. My whole body shook in horror, and I sobbed deeply. My throat was tight. My head ached. My chest pounded. I felt as though I had been thrown against a stone wall. For a long time I sat in silence until I heard my self say aloud, "My dad beat my mom." I finally could speak the brutal truth that I had hidden, even from myself. When I walked away from my family at sixteen, I thought I had left it all behind. And here it was, a legacy I could no longer ignore. Was it his death that freed me now to look at the pain and the loss? To begin to address what I had chosen to forget?

I had ignored those first years of my life and was too involved with my new life to want to pick up these painful pieces and try to make sense of them. I had found new meaning through my community and my ministry. Another six years passed without me giving much thought to the memories that erupted on that sunny day. I saw a therapist periodically but never had the courage to talk about the family violence.

I was successful in my work as secretary to the Superior General of the congregation, a position to which I was appointed in 1976, though I always questioned my competency. I judged myself and felt insecure in every aspect of my life. My inability to trust interfered with my relationships. I lived in limbo. My outward life proceeded fairly well, yet inside I was falling apart. On February 3, 1981, I wrote:

> *I feel so helpless right now—so undone, really. It's not anything I can easily describe; can't even get in touch with why it hurts so much. I know there is much anger inside of me—much frustration—lots of tears and sometimes hopelessness.*

I continued to believe that there was something wrong with me, even as I presented myself to the world as a person who had it all together. Who was I, really? What was the truth about me and my life? Later that year I wrote:

The truth in me can sometimes be so frightening—too scary to deal with—too threatening. So I hold it inside and it eats at me. I push it down and at any moment it can raise its ugly head and spark my anger. Sometimes the anger is turned in on me, and I get depressed for days, months. Other times it comes out inappropriately. I am so confused.

I prayed for help and went for counseling off and on. I read self-help books, attended workshops, participated in classes, including an assertiveness class. Nothing seemed to touch me in a way that made a difference. Something was missing, and I couldn't find whatever it was. What I did not do was address my childhood trauma. It had slipped back into obscurity where I was content to let it lie.

In the spring of 1981, I requested and received permission to go away to graduate school to get a master's degree in social work. At the time, I knew I needed some distance from my religious family and everyone I knew. Why I needed to do this was not obvious. Was it really to get away from my life or was it to find me? Those two years, which I address in another chapter, were transformative and, indeed, were about finding. They prepared me for the next part of my journey.

In May, 1984, I learned about the Edgewood Program associated with Mercy Hospital in St. Louis, Missouri, an inpatient treatment program for chemical dependents. I was particularly interested in their outpatient Family Program for family members. A good friend who was also raised with an alcoholic father, had participated in the program, and I was intrigued by the positive changes I saw in her attitude and behavior. She was now better at setting boundaries in our relationship and seemed more peaceful. I wanted the serenity and the clarity that accompanied the choices she made. She claimed that what helped her was the AA Twelve-Step Program, to which she was introduced when she went through the Family Program.

With permission from my superior, I registered for the Family Program and drove to Edgewood every day for the next two weeks. I sat in a circle of twenty other people and learned about the effects that alcohol and other drugs have on family members. We listened to each others' stories. Some included accounts of violent abuse, and I realized for the first time that I was not the only adult child who had grown up with family violence.

Now I understood why I felt bad and broken. They talked about shame. They gave a name to my persistent feelings of inferiority, worthlessness, unlovableness; my fear of self-exposure that required me to screen every thought and word and stifle the childhood spontaneity I saw in other children. In class, when I didn't understand something, I never raised my hand to ask for help because I was ashamed of being me. Nor did I raise my hand if I knew the answer because of my shame. I saw my classmates do this and wondered why I couldn't. I listened as they gave the answer that I knew. And then, I felt even worse, more broken.

As the Family Program proceeded, I could see how distorted beliefs like "you can't do anything right" held me back. It became clear to me why, when there was a decision to be made in the community, I always deferred to the other members. I now understood my compulsive need to please, to be perfect, to have order, and my tendency to minimize my own needs and my inability to set boundaries. I realized I was not bad, and I wasn't broken. These were the patterns of beliefs, thoughts, and behaviors that I had developed to survive an abusive environment. This flash of awareness hit me as I sat in that circle, several days into the program. At first I felt stunned—and then excited. I had found the last piece of a puzzle I had sought for years.

I wish I could say that things got better after this, but it got worse. The program's aftercare included weekly one-on-one counseling and group therapy. At first, I sat in silence because I am a private person. Each time I went to a session was an act of courage that I didn't know I had. The sessions were grueling, and I'll never forget the first one.

The group leader looked over at me. I squirmed in my chair and my stomach tightened. "So Helen, why don't you start." In my mind, I sorted through several situations from which to select something, but there was nothing. If only this were a game where I could pass. But they were are all waiting for my answer. I blurted out, "At times I feel like a balloon filled with flaming anger, and when it is touched, bits of that terrible stuff seeps out like some awful disease. I try to hold it back, but sometimes I wish it would all come out and be done with it."

"Why do you hold it back?" the woman sitting next to me asked.

"Because I'm afraid if I expressed what I feel, I couldn't stop. I would destroy everything around me."

The therapist observed what I already knew. "So your anger doesn't match what triggered it. What do you think the anger is about?" At this point it was difficult enough to admit my anger, much less claim its cause. Anger has always scared me.

I hesitated, but I needed to answer. "This has been growing in me since I was a kid. My dad was always angry. He abused my mother and manipulated all of us with his sick behaviors and with his anger. Mom was so preoccupied with him that she was unavailable to us emotionally. I know she did the best she could, but it left me crippled, and I'm angry about that. I'm angry about the fact that I have to spend my energies now figuring out what's wrong and how to fix my life. I'm angry with God because He never responded to my pleas for help as a child. I'm angry about the effect this has had on our family relationships. They're not good." I heard and felt the energy of my anger. So much for invisibility. In that moment, my heart and soul were laid bare for all to see, especially me.

One evening, I shared a situation with my therapy group that had triggered a deep resentment. At the last minute, a friend had asked me to go see a play with her. I preferred to stay home. Without expressing my preference, I chose to go. The entire time I was at the play, I kept thinking about what I could be doing at home. My friend noticed my silence.

"You're awfully quiet tonight, Helen. Are you okay?"

"I'm fine. Just concentrating on the story line."

Later she continued to question me, and I told her I was tired and tried to turn the conversation back to her. By the time the evening was over, I felt resentful, but I also felt like I had been dishonest.

A group member asked, "Why didn't you just tell her you wanted to stay home?"

"I knew she didn't want to go alone; I could let go of my preference."

"What were you afraid of, Helen?"

I didn't have to think long about this. "I was afraid she would be upset with me."

"So you don't like conflict?"

I thought about that and realized that I not only acted to avoid possible conflict; I also abandoned my own needs in order to avoid conflict. I abandoned myself. This is how I managed my life most of the time.

Participants in the Family Program were strongly encouraged to join Al-Anon and seek out a sponsor—which I dutifully did—even though it was agony at times for me to talk about myself, my thoughts, feelings, motivations, reactions. One of the unspoken messages I believed as a child was, *Don't feel, don't talk, don't trust.* I learned to ignore my feelings. I didn't have the words to talk about the violence I witnessed, even if I had wanted to. I trusted no one.

To learn to talk, trust, and access my feelings at age forty-three was an uphill battle for me. Though I attended weekly Al-Anon meetings, it was a full year before I opened my mouth, other than to say my name and claim that I was an adult child of an alcoholic. Every week, I sat and listened to the stories of courageous men and women who were trying to change their lives as they worked the Twelve Steps. In time, I risked my own self-revelation and talked about my struggle to let go of blaming my parents for how the family violence affected me. It was now up to me to change my responses to life, and I had The Twelve-Step program to guide my efforts to make these changes.

The process of change is tricky. At one point we find that we are no longer where we were, but we haven't quite reached where we are going. It is the disorienting part of the journey where we either choose to move on through the darkness or stay stuck. All the necessary elements were now in place for me to make that choice.

My relationship with God was stretched beyond the familiar image of some male Being way out there. This new Higher Power was more approachable, more relevant, and required me to be more responsible, less dependent. But I continued to feel disconnected and struggled to relate to God in a meaningful way that would make a difference in my life.

My relationship with myself was a new concept that emerged through the Family Program, Al-Anon, and readings about recovery. I understood that my inner, true self was that part of me that I had stifled and denied by my choices to believe those early distorted messages that I was bad, unlovable, and unworthy. This was reinforced by my failure to acknowledge my own needs and to, instead, please others. For years I had remained disconnected from that true part of me. Now I had the opportunity to get to know myself, but I would have to let go of the false self I had created and believe something very different.

My relationship with other people in my life challenged me. Now I needed to balance respect for them with respect for myself. I needed to express my needs and preferences, while at the same time honoring those of the other person. I needed to get past the fear of rejection and be more open in my communications. Above all, I had to trust that I could cope with whatever response came my way from the other person.

I thought I knew what I believed, but as I made changes in my life, I was thoroughly confused. How was I to believe that I was not responsible for meeting other people's needs? To believe that my feelings counted? To believe that the only control I had was to create my own reality by the choices I made? To believe that I even had a choice and did not always have to defer to the other?

As I went through these changes, there was a seismic shift in my life that threw me into the eye of a storm that wiped out whatever held my life together, and by the following year I was in a deep hole of depression. My days were shrouded in darkness that I could not escape. There was no ladder to the top. The inner work I was doing through therapy and Al-Anon stirred an ocean of rage that had accumulated since my childhood days, a product of my violent father and emotionally absent mother. I couldn't sleep. God was gone. I isolated myself from my community when I could. There were days when I walked into my office and simply stood there with no idea of where to start or what to do.

By this time, I had established the new position of Mission Coordinator for the SSM Health Care System. I worked with the CEO and employees of each facility to set up a Mission Committee that supported efforts to keep the mission and spirit of the sisters alive in their facility. This required nurturing a relationship with each facility's personnel through periodic visits to Madison,

Wisconsin; Blue Island, Illinois; Jefferson City, Missouri; and Dillon, South Carolina. I spent a great deal of my energy just doing the work. The little energy that remained didn't seem to be enough to maintain my personal well-being. I felt like I was losing my grip on life itself as I stood there in my office looking out on the tranquil grounds surrounding the building. I was so depressed that it didn't occur to me to call someone and ask for help.

Journal entry July 11, 1985:

> *Dear God, whoever you are, wherever you are,*
>
> *There is an emptiness in my life and a deadness. I really don't want to do anything, go anywhere. Since last May I have found myself in a desert, with no landmarks that I can recognize. I am feeling unrelated to anyone or anything. It's very dry. I feel isolated with only myself to behold. The self-knowledge I'm experiencing, especially through the Family Program, is very painful for me to accept. I am seeing things in myself that I don't want to claim as part of me. Yet, I know that they are mine. This is who I am. I see my brokenness, neurotic dependence, lack of integration, poor self-esteem. I feel lost and unsure of myself. There is nothing to hold on to, no sense of direction for me. Once I knew where to find answers. Now, in this cold, dark place there is nothing and no one to turn to.*
>
> *I feel like I've lost the language for speaking with you. You're too far away to hear anyway. I'm lost and tired of looking for you. You evade my every effort to reach you. Do you find me so distasteful to be with? Are you sorry you created me in the first place? I feel deserted and left by you, as if the relationship we had never existed. I've decided to stay right where I am in this desert. I will stop looking for you. I will not push myself to pray. I will sit when my body asks me to sit; lay when it wants to lay. I will not push myself to sing when there is no*

song. I will look at the stars only for their beauty as stars, not trying to see your eyes in them.

So find me, if you will God. Who knows the discoveries I may make sitting here in the middle of nowhere. Some day this darkness will end. I will survive. I will find a new way to be in this world. And you will find me.

Shortly after writing this note to God, I opened my favorite book of the Old Testament. I love the poetry of the Psalms for their varied responses to the human condition. In the past, I relished the verses that expressed joy and praise. Those that caught my attention at this time reeked of sorrow, angst, and despair. Psalm 88:15 said it all. *Why, oh Lord, do you reject me; why hide from me your face?*

The oppressive summer heat was not unlike the force that held me silent, even as the disowned, true part of me longed to be revealed. But I had no skills for coming out. By the fall of 1985, my inner battle spilled over into my community life. One October Sunday evening, we convened for our weekly community meeting and within moments each of my sisters confronted me with their concerns.

"Helen, I worry about your isolation and lack of participation in community activities."

"You seem so angry, Helen, but you keep it all in."

"I'm concerned for your safety, Helen. I was behind you the other day, and you were driving way too fast."

I listened without response. I was stunned by this turn of events. My thoughts spun; my pulse raced. They asked me if I was willing to get help. With reluctance I said, "Yes." One of the sisters left the room and called the hospital.

I took my bag from the closet shelf and opened it on my bed. What do you take with you to a psych unit? I'd never done this.

I couldn't grasp what was happening. Eventually, I threw in items that seemed foreign but maybe necessary: a novel, my Bible, a notebook, walking shoes, pajamas, a change of clothing. The context of my life was melting away. Nothing seemed relevant.

Within the hour, I was on my way to St. Mary's Health Center where I was admitted to the open psych unit. The staff took away everything that I had brought with me. I felt stripped of everything, including my identity. I was now the patient in room 134. I vacillated between not wanting to be there and feeling relieved that maybe now I would be purged of the badness that had plagued me since childhood. I didn't know what to expect or what I wanted or where this was going—or where I was going. I had never experienced such disorientation. It was the first time in my life that I completely let go because this was something I could not manage or control. And I had no God to turn to.

From my childhood days of trying to protect my little sisters until now, I had lived a life focused on taking care of others. The hospital environment was foreign and forbidding. I could take care of no one but myself. There was no escape from the self I did not know. My daily routine required self care, that I ask for what I needed, and talk about what was troubling me. This was unfamiliar territory. It was as though all the previous years of my life had been wiped out, and I would never be the same after this. I was back in first grade, starting all over. Only this time, I had some major decisions to make before I could move on.

There was a lot not to like about my two-week hospital stay, notably, the lack of privacy. It was also the first time in my life that I was without any responsibility. I felt lighter in this strange space. Everything was unpredictable, especially the number of people who visited me daily. The nurses threatened to put a No Visitor sign on my door, but I resisted. These visits were the most healing part of my experience. At first, I felt awkward as I sat with a co-worker or friend or hospital staff.

"So, Sister, how are you? We're all praying for you."

Behind my smile, I wondered: does s/he know why I'm here? "I'm feeling much better, thank you. Sleeping better; seeing my psychiatrist every day. And how are you? How's your family?"

With a few close friends I shared in-depth—questions about where my life was going; what I would do when I left the hospital. I needed to resign my position at the corporate office. Sometimes I cried with my visitor, no longer able to hide my sadness and persistent aloneness. Despite the outpouring of love and care, which was new for me, I was on an inward journey, and no one else could go with me.

I feel lonelier now than I've ever felt as an adult. Perhaps it's the same loneliness I felt as a child—when I wandered alone and chose to stay away from everyone because no one really cared or even noticed what was happening to me. I remember how much that hurt. Whether I was absent from the playground or from a family situation—it didn't seem to matter to anyone. All along there was the growing conviction that I was no good, undesirable, uninteresting, that I was in the way most of the time, unloved. Just tolerated.

My stay in the hospital and the months that followed were a powerful turning point. I allowed myself to feel cared for and loved. While the walls within me were breaking down, I began to set boundaries in little ways that would, in time, change the direction of my life. I asked and received permission from my superior to move out of the small community where we lived near St. Mary's Hospital and live alone in an apartment for a year. I needed to learn who I was as a person separate from my religious family. I resigned my position as Mission Coordinator, and after a period of recuperation, went in search of a job.

Through the Twelve-Step program and therapy, which I continued into 1986, I saw how long-standing beliefs and behaviors that had helped me survive my violent home environment now limited me. Back then, I needed to be invisible, to not speak up but blend in. I knew that if I accommodated and pleased others, I would be safe. My discomfort with the constant conflict and chaos led me to seek comfort by creating order in my external environment to an extreme degree.

These and many other coping skills no longer worked. These patterns covered the pain I needed to heal. Healing is about change, which was only possible after I acknowledged and accepted who I was with my brokenness, as well as my strengths. I could not begin to change until I first met and accepted the real Helen, the child who was first emotionally abandoned by Mom and subsequently abandoned by me, the adult. I had to be honest with myself and others, beginning with my sponsor.

Journal entry December 1, 1985:

> *I have reached a crossroad in my life. This depression has stopped me in my tracks. I have had to let go, to listen, to receive, to be, and to discover that I am loved. I have had two months away from work and time to re-evaluate myself and where I am going. I'm scared, I'm relieved, I'm excited about new possibilities. I'm learning the importance of facing the truth; being honest—which means dealing with my co-dependency.*
>
> *What is the truth of what I'm moving toward? Where is this process leading me? What will happen if I let myself ask these questions? Is it worth the risk? Will the people now in my life still be there for me if I should choose to change my lifestyle? Where is my higher power in all this? Am I making this all happen? Or is it meant to be? It seems that a process has begun—things have happened, people have come along—I've been challenged to look at all aspects of my life differently—and here I am, faced with questions that didn't exist a few months ago.*

The answers did not come easily. The winter of 1985 was dark and foggy. I felt lost again, but this time my inner eyes were open, and I was straining to see where I was going. My greatest obstacle was the fact that I had long ago learned to block out my feelings, one of the most important tools we have to figure out what's really going on inside of us.

Journal entry December 25, 1985:

What am I feeling? I have a hard time getting in touch with what I feel. I want to know what I feel and respond accordingly. Something blocks me. Maybe it's just an old pattern that I can't let go of. It feels uncomfortable – like it doesn't fit anymore. The feeling I struggle with the most is anger. I resist expressing my anger. I think this is because I can't believe that anger can co-exist with love, acceptance, goodness, and security. As a child, when I was angry with my father for the mean, violent things he did, I hid my anger. I had to be OK with him, no matter what. How could I be angry with this person whose love I didn't want to lose? And besides, I had learned that to be angry is to be violent and destructive. I couldn't do that. Being good meant not being angry.

For so long I have controlled my feelings according to others' expectations because of the need to survive, to be loved and accepted. Now I want to be Helen but I can't sort out what/who is me and what/who is the other. It will get clearer, I hope.

By January, 1986, I felt challenged to let go of the denial that had governed my life all these years. I wanted to live more in tune with my truth, whatever that was. This was a year of discovery filled with uncertainty. I was forty-five years old and had never lived alone; I had never written a resume or hunted for a job. My new one-bedroom apartment took shape with odds and ends that were given to me or borrowed. I learned that my favorite colors were green and lavender and used them to brighten my tiny bathroom.

As I looked for a job, balanced my meager budget, and created new routines, I faced, for the first time, the distorted self I had created at an early age, the self I hated and denied. Through this new living situation and with the support of several friends, I gradually began to look at myself with different eyes. But at the end of the day, I was there, alone—alone with the confusion of not being where I used to be and not yet where I was going. Though God and I still were not on friendly terms, out of habit more than anything, I expressed my loneliness to the One to whom I had turned for as long as I could remember.

Journal entry January 29, 1986:

> O God! I am so lonely tonight! Notice I'm not asking where you are. You are everywhere I am not. There is a vacuum in my soul in which I am suspended. I reach out screaming for someone and there is no response. I kick and knock about in the darkness, trying to touch something—anything. But there is only blankness.
>
> I am filled with tears, you know. There is a river inside me, about to overflow. O God, why have you forsaken me? Why can I not hear or see—or feel an arm around me?
>
> Tell me I am wrapped in self-pity—it's true. I'm feeling sorry for myself. But look—just peer into this darkness with me. And tell me—what do _you_ feel?
>
> I am falling, falling—swirling as I drop into the depths of my being. Is there no bottom to this timeless pit? Is there no end to this space-less place?
>
> I tell myself to be calm, be still—just let your self feel the pain of being alone. Don't seek to fill this empty space inside

your heart. Let it be in its emptiness. Don't rush the time of understanding it—so that you can get to know the whole of it—YOUR heart.

OK—so I will wait—until it's hollowness echoes the searing, searching pain and anger I find so impossible to express. And then what? Must I wait forever for that moment when it will fill again with peace and joy and loveliness, without the strain?

Tonight I reacted defensively—like so many times before—to some innocent event. I'm not sure why. I think it's the anger that will not go away but surges up each chance it gets, spoiling my words with its ugliness. And then I felt so bad—why did I do that. Why am I so bad? Why can't I just be the self I want to be?

I think it's the overwhelming pain that eats at me, the silent anger that seethes through ever fiber of my being—yet will not be outspoken in its truth because the price to be paid is one I cannot yet pay. There are so many things I'm afraid to say.

In time I will stand my space—and with my heart, blurt out what in that moment I am feeling, regardless of the pain it must surely cause. In time I will tell you exactly who I am and what I need and where I am going—and what I will not do and where I will not go. I'll be dammed if I will sell my soul to please you or anybody else!

Be still in your loneliness, my heart; listen to the faint strain of music that is your song—and start softly to sing it with all your might.

Twenty-seven years later, I realize that this was my declaration of independence. It redirected my journey and loosened the grip the effects of family violence had on me. As I began to live my declaration, I had a clearer sense of direction in my life, but was not prepared for where it would lead me.

In the early 1980s, I was aware of a theme that ran in the background of my life. It was a sense that something was shifting within me that did not fit with the life to which I had committed myself as a nun. Because of this commitment, I had refused to allow myself to even ask the questions that emerged at times. I felt so sure I was where I belonged. I loved my community, my sisters, our mission, and the lifestyle. I knew I had been called to this life. I couldn't believe that I would be called out of it. I had no other plans. I knew I would never marry. That was a decision I had made a long time ago as a little girl when I promised myself I would never put myself in my mother's position. But like other issues in my life, I eventually had to face this one.

In December of 1986, I went into a weekend retreat to pray and ask for guidance. I needed to make a decision because by now my inclination to leave the congregation was growing stronger. I didn't sleep the first two nights. The decision I had to make haunted me as I walked among the barren trees in the retreat center garden. I sorted through the years of my life with the Sisters of St. Mary and all the reasons I should remain. And then I wrestled with the evidence that I had changed—deeply—in these past five years. If I continued as a member, I could not be true to the self I had become, and to do otherwise would be one more abandonment of Helen.

The morning of the third day, I wrote a letter to my superior, Sister Mary Ellen, with the reasons I needed to request a dispensation from my vows. A profound sadness engulfed me as I penned the letter I never thought I would write. This was matched by an overwhelming sense of peace that gave me the strength to proceed, a peace about my decision that has never left me. Even so, I had no idea where I was going, what I would do, or how I would manage my life.

This was the most painful decision I had ever made as an adult. It meant that I would walk away from people I had lived with since my teen years, women whose lives had inspired, challenged, and supported me. These were my closest friends, my family, and I had given my life to them. We were bound together in love and in service. But I had to go. I did not fully comprehend the changes within me; I just knew that if I stayed, I could not continue to grow personally in the way I needed to. I would languish.

I finalized my decision on a cold, gray day. The retreat house chapel where I knelt for hours was damp and dreary with nothing to offer comfort but the little candle burning bright near the tabernacle. I was very small when I first learned that the lit candle in that space signified the presence of the Eucharist. So many times during grade school, when my father's violence ravaged our family life, I spent my recess time sitting in the front pew of the church where I felt close to God and safe because of that little dancing flame on the altar.

In the weeks that followed, I met with the members of my small community and each of my closest peers to talk with them about my decision. I wanted them to know that I planned to leave and why. Their responses varied. Some remained silent with not much to say. Others expressed anger or questioned how I could do this. My best friend stopped all communication with me. I was not prepared for such anger and total lack of support. But in the midst of all of this, I never doubted that I had made a good decision.

My formal dispensation had to come from the Vatican. I received it within a few months of my request. The documents were written in Latin, but I understood that I had been released from my vows. I left my religious family during the bleakness of March, 1987.

The finality of my dispensation was at first a heavy cloud that settled over me and filled me with a sense of deep, agonizing loss that was not eased by the knowledge that I had made the right choice. I felt sad, really sad. My days were empty without my sisters to go home to. My heart ached with loneliness when I thought of what I left behind: my sisters, my community, and a way of life that I cherished. It was all so good, and such a significant part of who I had become. I was a ship cut loose from its moorings, moving out to sea with no certain destination.

In time, I began to make new friends and discover ways to create a new life for myself. With the help of a friend, I found a job at a local hospital as the social worker on a chemical dependency unit. I began to reconnect with my own family that I had left behind twenty-seven years ago. They had changed, as had I. We no longer knew each other. It took some time for us to reconnect at a meaningful level. What hurt the most was that when I left my religious family, I was totally cut off from them. It was ten years before I was invited back to share a meal with my sisters.

The 1980s was my decade of death and resurrection. Eventually, I expanded the network of people in my life, both personally and professionally. I studied, practiced, and taught the truths and skills I had learned along the way, and I met other women who, like me, were deeply wounded by family violence. Most of them were not aware that their current difficulties were directly related to the patterns of belief and behaviors they had developed in their effort to survive. Even less obvious was the fact that, in the midst of all their trauma and struggle, they had also developed skills that could be honed and modified to support a new way of life. We who have survived family violence use what we've learned to become resilient victors, no longer victims.

Journey Into Loneliness

(Journal entry January 25, 1986, 1:30am)

There is a journey we each must take
at some point in our lives.
   I think I've begun—it feels like loneliness.

Some months ago I asked "how long is forever?"
The answer is not an easy one, and yet,
   I know it is inside of me—it feels like loneliness.

I've finished part of my forever, somehow it's behind me.
It's time to start anew, like starting over.
   I'm ready now to be with Me—it feels more real.

My best friend walked away from me a month ago,
unable to bear the pain of changes I'm about
   I miss her desperately—it feels like rejection and loss.

My community has cared about me up to a point.
Now they want me to behave and continue as before.
   I know they can't understand or accept my pain—it feels
like a closed door.

I have little energy to nurture other relationships.
I'm afraid to be vulnerable in their presence.
   They may register disappointment in me—it feels lonely
here.

And so I stand alone beneath the stars of darkness.
The Universe seems unaware of me and where I am.
   This journey leads me down a silent path—it feels so
unfamiliar.

My heart longs to know the melody of my song,
so as to sing of me and not the song of someone else.
   The tune is faint but coming stronger to my ears—it sounds
like me.

The journey into loneliness need not end in despair,
if through it I can find myself, and finally care.
  In the dark coolness of my being—it feels so right.

There is no turning back upon this path
In darkness I trust my lone companion—me.
  There is a breath of life in moments when—I am OK with me.

This journey into loneliness is teaching me
I cannot expect to find the support I need,
  except within myself—where love resides.

O darkness you cannot hide the life I am
But rather, force me to let it be and shine.
  Less lonely will I be—attuned to Me.

Chapter Nineteen

EMBRACING THE ABANDONED SELF

*We do not believe in ourselves until someone reveals that
deep inside us something is valuable, worth listening to,
worthy of our trust, sacred to our touch. Once we believe
in ourselves, we can risk curiosity, wonder, spontaneous
delight or any experience that reveals the human spirit.*

—e.e.cummings

Weeks before I was to start eighth grade, my father took my sisters and me from our home in rural Washington County, Missouri to the city of St. Louis and dropped us off with an aunt we did not know. We were supposed to live there until our parents worked out the details of our permanent move to accommodate my dad's new job. We had no idea when we would see our parents again. Days before this traumatic move, I found an abandoned baby rabbit in the field near Grandma's house. A horse had apparently stepped in the hole that held the nest. None of its littermates survived. I put the little bunny in an old birdcage and nursed it with milk and an eye dropper. When we got to my aunt's house, I smuggled our little caged bunny upstairs. My aunt was a gruff woman, so we were sure she would not allow us to keep it.

A steep, narrow stairway led to the second floor room that would be our home for an unknown period of time. It was vacant, except for an old bare mattress on the floor that was just wide enough for the three of us. Aunt Flo scowled as she handed me a couple of sheets and a pillow. The floors were uneven and the linoleum was cracked and worn. There were no curtains on the small, dusty windows. A single, naked light bulb hung from the ceiling.

That first month of school was agonizing. It was clear that my sisters and I were an imposition to this family who did not want us there. I had full responsibility for the girls as we transitioned into a new school and a class culture that was far advanced beyond the rural environment we had known. Every day I wondered when we would see our mom and dad again.

We named the little orphan bunny Nibbles. He was our only fun distraction from the isolation and homesickness we felt. After the evening meal, we would sit on the mattress and let Nibbles out of his cage, each taking a turn to hold and pet him. Eventually, he could eat grass from the yard that I gathered and stuffed in my schoolbag after school. And then one day, I knew we had to let Nibbles go because he had grown too big for the cage that had protected and supported his survival. One night after dark, when the family downstairs had gone to bed, I carried the cage, and we crept down the stairs and out to the backyard. I opened the door and released Nibbles into the yard, a barren space that had a few patches of grass, some wild weeds growing tall around an old oak tree, and a few scraggly bushes. My sisters and I stood beside the empty cage and cried as we watched our bunny scamper off into the bushes. Like us, Nibbles had no one now. I felt so responsible and so alone.

The next day, as I walked across the schoolyard, my teacher, Sister Adelbert, caught up with me and put her arms around my shoulders. "How are you doing, Helen?" She said this with such sincerity that I wanted to turn and throw myself into her arms. As I write this almost sixty years later, a lump grows in my throat, and I am tearful. I remember how sad I was then and how much I needed that hug. She had no idea how starved for affection I was. "I'm fine, sister," was all I could say. That single moment when I felt her care sustained me through the remainder of that heavy time of isolation and is still alive in me today. I have passed that hug on many times since, each an act of connection and concern.

If I could choose only one message to write upon your heart, it would be this: We must recognize that we are all connected—with each other and with our environment. This sense of relatedness is essential for our healing, wholeness, and serenity. As the earth needs the sun, so we need each other. We cannot grow, survive, or thrive without each other. When we feel connected to one another, we have a sense that we are accepted, we belong, and we are safe. That's it. This interpersonal connection creates the environment we need to accept ourselves, to reconnect with our true self and transcend our brokenness. Our relatedness makes transformation possible.

Whether the dysfunction we grew up with was alcohol or drug abuse, mental illness, or family violence, the adults in those situations could not see and value the innate goodness of their children, much less reflect it back to us. Consequently, we grew up focused on survival in a situation where no one even acknowledged the abuse that robbed us of our childhood. We believed that we were deficient, guilty, powerless, responsible, and unworthy. There was no one to correct these distorted perceptions and interpretations of ourselves and our reality. We were filled with shame, were hyper-vigilant and poor at play. We were disconnected from our true emotions, and therefore, from ourselves. Without the benefit of our blocked feelings and the safety to express them, we learned to ignore, disclaim, or deny our needs, wants, and preferences—our very selves.

So with this complicated past, where do we start if we want to learn to embrace the self we have abandoned, especially when we feel so unworthy of that embrace? Eventually, we need to experience what we didn't experience as a child. Someone must care enough about us to recognize our value and communicate that care in a way that we actually *feel* valued and cared for. Because we have a distorted perception of ourselves, we can't see our own value, so it must be reflected back to us through a connection someone offers. It may be as simple as a smile, a word of encouragement, an act of kindness, or a loving arm around our shoulder.

I recall such moments of connection, and realize that this is what helped me feel good enough to take the next step. Each choice I made toward believing that I was a person of value meant that I could, in time, transcend my painful story of family violence and its effects that I carried into my adult life. Although these once debilitating effects, including my thought and behavior patterns, are still a part of who I am and still surface periodically in my current life, the terrifying experience of growing up in a violent home no longer defines me. To grow beyond all this, to be transformed, I had to acknowledge my father's abuse and claim the fear it generated in me and in my family. Because I grew up in survival mode, I learned to respond to life out of fear. Once I claimed this experience, I was free to find the help I needed to make healthier choices and reclaim the self I had abandoned.

It took many years for me to make the changes that transformed me, due partly to the fact that, for a long time, I was without guidance. From the moment I left home, I knew I had to make it on my own. It never occurred to me to ask for help, not for anything. I was the one who helped others, the one who took care of whatever was needed. I selected my own senior high school classes and arranged to take them by correspondence courses through a school in Chicago. I found my own job at St. Mary's Hospital. I arranged for my own housing, which consisted of a room that I shared with my cousin at St. Elizabeth Hall. This was an apartment building for single working women that was run by the Sisters of St. Mary. I struggled through the perils of dating for the first time, and I made my own decision about what I would do when I graduated high school—all without asking anyone for guidance.

I had worked at the hospital for almost a year and was about to receive my high school diploma when I decided to join the Sisters of St. Mary. They came to know me through my work and periodic visits to the convent. One day, when I was at the convent getting measured for the habit I would soon wear, Mom called St. Elizabeth Hall to talk with me and was told that I was at the convent. That Friday, my parents picked me up to go home with them for the weekend. I sat quietly in the back of our old Plymouth and wondered how to tell them that I was going to join the convent. For the past week, I had tried to prepare myself for my father's blowup. Halfway home, I blurted out, "I'm resigning my job at the end of the month." Before anyone could say anything, I added, "And I'm taking July off because in August, I plan to join the Sisters." Silence. I knew Mom was thinking about the family bills I had agreed to pay off.

Finally, my dad spoke with a softness he seldom displayed. "Well, if that's what you think will make you happy, okay."

I had not asked for his blessing, but I was relieved to receive it. They wanted to know the date and time of the entrance ceremony. Nothing more was said about the matter. I was about to enter a life that would remove me from my family for the rest of my days, a life about which we knew very little, and yet, we did not talk about it. For the rest of the weekend, it was as if nothing had happened. So many questions, so much finality to my decision to live such a different life, and I needed to talk about it, to know what they thought. Did they have concerns for me? Did they really understand what I was doing? The silence that hung over us was heavier because of what it held, including my need to know what my life choice meant to them.

I had very little contact with my family or the outside world for the first two and a half years of my new life, no access to radio, TV, or newspaper. This intense period of formation was a time to focus on the study of the rule of St. Francis along with the history and customs of the Congregation. Each day was strictly structured with the discipline of work, prayer, and study, followed by evening recreation. Our class consisted of sixteen women, ages fourteen to forty-something, all of us intent upon learning how to live in community. I missed my little sisters, but found it easy to adapt to my new home and family.

The second phase of my formation took place during the next four years while I attended college at St. Louis University and worked at St. Mary's hospital. Now I had access to the news and was able to follow developments of the Vietnam War, when I could get my hands on a newspaper. I sympathized with the protest against the war. The pictures were horrifying. I cut out one photo of a soldier who carried a little boy who had been shot and kept it on my desk to remind me that the soldier and the victim were my brothers. My world continued to expand when, in 1966, I made my final vows, graduated from St. Louis University with a bachelor's degree in medical record administration, and traveled to several of the system's hospitals to assist temporarily in the record department. I received my first permanent assignment in 1967.

The 1960s were in full swing, and the winds of change swirled through society, the church, and even my congregation. I was in my early twenties, fully absorbed in my role as a hospital department head with responsibilities that demanded skills I had yet to learn. I was challenged, both personally and professionally, and felt good that I was able to meet the challenges, though not without my share of mistakes and blunders. I knew nothing about hiring and evaluating employees, felt intimidated by the doctors, and had to determine criteria for ordering medical books for the library. I had never prepared for a committee meeting or developed a departmental budget. The job required me to interact with a multitude of people at many different levels of the organization, along with the twenty-five sisters with whom I lived. I had never been so immersed in so many relationships at the same time. My old survival patterns emerged and took over. I was a people-pleaser and a perfectionist and needed to be in control, yet be invisible. My challenge was to learn to respond in a new way. Unfortunately, I had not yet recognized these patterns, nor did I know how to deal with them.

Society, the church, and the congregation slid into the chaos of the 1960s, and I fell into my own deep, personal turmoil about which I had no insight. Depressed, overwhelmed, and confused, I tried to hide my anguish from my community, with whom I felt little connection. One day, I was so desperate that I did something I had never done: I asked for help. I called Sister Marion, who had a compassionate heart and a degree in psychology. Though I didn't know her well, I believed she would keep my confidence. When we met, I cried more than I talked, and that seemed to be a great relief in itself. My feelings were too deep for words. Issues swirled around inside me that I did not recognize. Marion listened to me and her care softened my heart. I never returned for another session, but a smidgen of my fear had been replaced with a smidgen of trust. I knew that if I wanted to break out of my miserable isolation, something had to change. I needed to face my inner struggles, and I needed help. It would be some time before I sought that help.

In the meantime, the Second Vatican Council (1963–1965) had produced sixteen documents that would change the course of the Church and our Congregation. Our superiors were serious about these new directives, especially those that addressed Religious Life and the Laity, and they gradually introduced numerous changes. Prior to this time, the leadership did not consult us about major changes they would make. Now we were involved, and the first noticeable change we made was the modification of the length and style of the habit we wore. In time, we were each given $25 a month for personal expenses. We were allowed to visit our families at home, something previously allowed only in emergencies. For the first time ever, we were allowed to take vacations. There were other changes that helped us enhance our spiritual lives and our ministry.

One of the biggest changes to which we had to adapt was the move from living in communities of fifteen to twenty members, into smaller communities of five to eight. I could no longer remain invisible. I lived with four sisters now, not twenty. I was forced to be in relationships, to get to know the others and be known by them. I had to be a visible participant in community life, accountable as an individual and as a group member. I felt catapulted out of a known, traditional, safe structure into a spotlight I had always tried to avoid.

This overall process of updating religious life was too drastic for some of our members, and a significant number chose to leave. It was a painful time for us and for most of the other religious communities.

Five of us lived in a house several blocks from the hospital where we worked. I enjoyed the solitary walk home at the end of the day because I had time alone to think. One day shortly after we moved in, I spent my walk time obsessing over the meal I would prepare when I got home. It was my turn to cook, something I had never learned to do. I was already anxious but my insecurity was heightened by the fact that the other four were good cooks.

"What is that smell?" Sara asked as she walked into the house. I had just taken the charred meatloaf from the oven and was about to panic. She smiled at me, took the pan and put it in the sink. "Let's see if any of it is salvageable." When she turned to look at me, I knew the verdict. "You really did it in," she said in a way that lightened the moment.

"I feel terrible, Sara. What are we going to do for dinner?" I asked.

"It's no big deal," she replied. "There's a pizza in the freezer. I'll make a salad. You get rid of the carcass before the others get home."

I learned a lot in those moments—about Sara, about me, and about alternative ways to respond to undesirable circumstances. Sara had a knack for easing any situation. I soon learned that each of us had something special to offer.

That evening we sat at table and talked about our day. One advantage of living in a smaller group was the opportunity to share and feel each other's supportive presence. Since I still didn't have much trust, I shared cautiously. I did want my housemates to know that I had planned to serve something better than pizza. When I told them what happened to the meatloaf, they laughed and each had a story to tell about their first cooking experience. Later at evening prayer, we all had something to be grateful for. My gratitude was for this community where I felt accepted without judgment, cared about, and respected. I felt so free, so safe, truly embraced. This was a new experience for me and one that continued throughout my days in community.

I'm not sure which came first for me, trusting others or allowing myself to be embraced and then trusting. In time, I learned some of what it meant to embrace another person: be with, listen, allow, get to know, respect, trust, and respond. I still had a long way to go in terms of embracing myself, especially that part of me that I rejected.

One sister, who recognized that I was overly-critical of myself, tried repeatedly to affirm and encourage me. One sunny Saturday afternoon, I worked my way through a basket of laundry and listened to all the reasons she thought I should get more involved in community activities. "You have so much to offer, Helen. You're smart and wise. You're experienced, and you have a lot of feeling. You're compassionate and helpful."

I folded the last towel slowly and without looking up, asked her "How do you know all this? You don't really know me." The truth was that I didn't want her to know me, and I certainly didn't believe any of what she said. After that, I tried to avoid her, but in time, I started to think that she might be right. Eventually we became friends, but because we both grew up with alcoholic fathers, we each had a strong need to control the relationship. Our co-dependent natures created continuous conflict that we weathered for twenty-plus years.

Whenever we disagreed, my initial reaction was to give in to her. I made little effort to communicate my own position. I thought she was smarter than me and that if I disagreed with her, she might abandon me. Once when I was away at graduate school, she called me to talk about an issue that troubled her. She said she wanted my input but then rejected whatever I offered her. I eventually tried to end the call but was unsuccessful. My strong need to rescue her blinded me to the fact that she really wanted my attention and didn't want me to abandon her. When I got my phone bill that month, there was a $60 charge for the call, a stinging reminder of my inability to set boundaries.

We were quite different from one another. She could be direct and say whatever was on her mind. I was indirect and passive, afraid to reveal what I was thinking. She was able to express her thoughts and feelings; I was not. She was not afraid to be herself, to be real. I dared not show myself. As she grew in insight and made the effort to change, she challenged me to speak my truth and to feel good about who I was. There were sporadic times when I attempted to be myself—and I did feel more real—but it would be years before I would realize that I had never lived my own life. Rather, I lived a life that I hoped would guarantee that

I was accepted. I had abandoned myself so that others wouldn't abandon me.

My friend and I both made our share of mistakes, but I cherish our experience of getting to know each other as we muddled through our relationship. We were both broken, but we wanted to learn and to heal.

During this transformative time in my life, I began to see that I had empty places in my heart and distorted beliefs about myself. If I didn't change these beliefs, they would entrap me in painful relationships, and my heart would remain forever empty.

As a child, I believed that if I did everything perfectly, my father would be pleased and then everything would get better. I desperately wanted to please him. Perfectionism and people-pleasing became survival skills that I have yet to uproot, though they have diminished as I've grown older. These patterns of belief were still very strong when, in my mid-thirties, I was appointed to the position of Secretary General—secretary to the Superior General of the Congregation. This was a responsibility and a privilege I never expected. Nor was I prepared for such an intense and demanding boss.

As it turned out, my new boss was more of a perfectionist than me. I was not an experienced typist, but I prided myself on many other skills that fit the position. Almost every document I typed for her that first month was returned to me if it had even the tiniest of errors. I worked on a typewriter, usually with multiple carbon copies, so often the entire document had to be retyped. What self-confidence I initially had faded, while my anxiety level shot through the roof. The old messages played in my head: *You can't do anything right; you're not good enough.* At the end of the day, I went home frustrated and defeated and was sure I would be fired the next day. My typing skills gradually improved and I remained at the job for six years until I asked permission to go away to graduate school.

This situation, where I was expected to perform with perfection and likewise expected it of myself as a means of pleasing someone in authority, was a wake-up call. I began to scrutinize the source and the effects of the distorted belief that I had to be perfect, and came to understand that I could only do my very best and must do that first to my own satisfaction. And, of course, I couldn't control another person's responses, no matter how much I tried to please or be perfect. Likewise, striving for perfection was no guarantee that I would be safe and accepted, as I thought when I was a child. I was tired of trying to be perfect and trying to please everyone else.

Years would pass before I understood that these behaviors were deeply rooted in beliefs I formed as a small child and held on to at the subconscious level. No matter what I learned and understood intellectually as an adult, to change a behavior, I had to identify, accept, and change the root belief. I could not do this without help because such a change must happen at every level: emotional, psychological, spiritual, and physical.

As a little girl, my job was to pull weeds in the garden. I soon learned that if I pulled off the visible part of the weed and left the roots intact, it would return in full strength before the week was over. During my thirties, I pulled a lot of weeds and struggled with the roots and had some successes. I studied, reflected, and attended workshops to help myself change troublesome behaviors such as my tendency to minimize my own needs. I practiced what I learned, but soon I was back to my old behavior. The root belief was still intact. Some were difficult to change.

During those years, I drove myself hard. I was at work by 7:00 a.m. and went back most evenings after dinner until 10:30 p.m. I never considered my need for rest, socialization, and recreation. I would readily pass up breaks or lunch to attend to someone else's need, and I made myself available 24/7. I grew up with the belief that to have needs, and to take time to attend to them, was the mark of a selfish woman. I also believed that working myself to exhaustion was one more way to express my perfection. A major burn-out experience and hospitalization in my forties finally made me stop and examine why I was living this way. My first morning in the hospital, I sat in a tiny conference room across from the psychiatrist and one of the first things he said was, "Sister, I want you to do one thing while you are here. Let the staff take care of you." I will never forget how foreign those words sounded to me, and how ready I was to do that.

By the time I got through my thirties, I had survived significant changes that had left a few bruises on my heart but also softened it. I had separated from my family, completed university and my first mission, had my first experience of falling in love, suffered a deep depression, experienced my dad's death, and received a major appointment in the Congregation. I had begun to get a glimpse of some of my inner strengths.

After six years as Secretary General, I asked permission to resign my position to pursue a Master's degree in Social Work. About to turn forty, I packed the old Chevy Citation the community loaned me and headed for Memphis, Tennessee to start graduate school at the University of Tennessee. For the next two years, I lived in a community of five women, all members of different religious communities. It was like moving away from a family that cared about me, but also knew my every shortcoming, and judged me on the basis of expectations I had not met. Every community, like a family, has its rules and traditions to which members are expected to conform. Being away from all that was such a relief. Here, I began with a clean slate. No judgments, just the expectation that I would be a supportive, participative community member. If I didn't show up for morning prayer periodically, it was not a problem.

My first school Practicum assignment was to work with the chaplain in a local hospital. Prior to this, I had worked in hospitals for twenty-plus years, so this was not the challenging assignment I had hoped for. However, I knew from my first meeting with the Chaplain and his assistant that I had lessons to learn there. Judy described the project she had planned, a stress reduction program for the hospital employees. I could help her.

"So when do we start?" I asked excitedly. Care for the employees was a strong priority of mine.

"I will be doing the program next week," she said. "You can help by collating the materials for the participants."

During those first weeks she gave me menial tasks to do, none of which provided the experience that would make this Practicum meaningful. I wanted to make it a better experience.

"Judy, can I make some of those phone calls for you? What if I helped with one of the booths during your workshop?" I asked.

"I don't know" she answered. "Let me think about it. Here, take this form to the emergency room."

As the days went by, Judy seemed threatened by my presence, as if she might lose control of the department. I did not have the skills to address her defensiveness, and as a result, my own insecurities grew. I found myself walking on eggshells, just like I had done as a child around my father. I finally got tired of this dynamic, and one day I asked if we could talk.

"Is there something I'm doing that bothers you?" I asked Judy. "If so, please tell me."

She seemed surprised at my directness, as was I. "No, you're fine" she answered. "I just don't know where I stand with my boss and my evaluation is coming up. I've never done a stress workshop, and I want it to go well."

"Then let me help you," I offered.

We did a lot more talking after that, and our communications improved. Judy realized that I was not the threat she thought I might be. By the time I completed my Practicum, we had come to appreciate each other, and I had a new sense of how to identify and work out some of my own insecurities.

My second assignment was in the prison system. I worked with first-time offenders, most of whom were black men aged eighteen or younger and who were on a track that would eventually lead to incarceration. The judge offered them an option. If they participated in the counseling program, their records would be expunged. Their lives were very different than mine, and they knew it. This dichotomy, coupled with my new role as a counselor, made for a real challenge. Some of the men weren't motivated to make meaningful changes, but one particular client was different. Though Zack tried his best and did his homework, he often missed his counseling session.

One day I asked, "Zack, what's the problem? You know that if you miss too many sessions, you could be dropped from the program. I'm concerned about you."

He slumped in his chair, and his eyes focused on a coffee stain in the worn carpet. He was quiet for a few moments. Then he looked up, and I saw confusion and sadness on his face. "I have a part-time job that I'm trying to hold on to. Things are rough at home. I need to get my GED," he answered.

"That's a lot for you to deal with, Zack. Can you tell me about home?"

His eyes re-focused on the carpet spot.

"Zack, I'd like to visit your home to meet your family. Would that be okay?" I asked.

"Sure. When?" he responded. I checked my schedule. "How about Friday?"

Zak's home was poorly lit, and his aging parents sat on a sofa, worn and spotted with use. Zack offered me a folding chair and then perched on the arm of the sofa, attentive to his dad who strained to hear the conversation. We talked about their living situation, multiple health issues, Zack's job, and their fear that he might go to prison. I struggled to maintain my composure as I tried to listen to his mother and not focus on a large roach as it crawled over my right foot. Clearly, the family needs were overwhelming. Zack needed more help than counseling.

Monday, I made a referral for a case manager to follow up with the family and determine what services might be available to them. The next time I met with Zack, I explained the service that I had requested for him and his family.

"But you've got to do the work of this program," I told him. "If you want to have your record cleared, you've got to get here for all your sessions. Do you understand?"

To set such a firm boundary was new to me and ever so difficult. I prayed for guidance and trusted that when I held Zak accountable to his counseling commitment, he would respond. That's exactly what happened, and I think part of his willingness was the result of my effort to look at his entire life situation and show concern for him as a person.

Zack was a success story, but in this practicum experience I often felt scared and alone, physically and emotionally. My supervisor was rarely available, and when I finally connected with her, she seemed distant and disinterested, with little to offer. She appeared burned out. At the same time, I learned important lessons and discovered more about who I was and what I could do. Best of all, I began to trust the self that I had abandoned.

I was excited about my future as a social worker and a psychotherapist. I learned so much from the people I met along the way, some of whom were phenomenal teachers. I also learned from the women I lived with, two of whom are still good friends.

Living in community was not without its lessons. One sister, at least ten years my senior, was often distant toward me and at times irritable. Her interactions with other community members were far more positive. Because I was afraid of conflict, I chose to ignore her behavior toward me, but in time it became unbearable.

One day, she exploded at me. I stood, shocked and shaken as she yelled at me.

"Who do you think you are? You go to school, but you don't have a job! What do you do with your time? When I was in school, I had to work full-time and carry a full load at university."

I couldn't speak, couldn't say a single word in response. A few days later, she walked into the kitchen and asked if we could talk. Every muscle in my body went into full alert and she must have seen the puzzlement in my eyes when I turned from the stove where I was cooking to look at her. Wishing for some way to escape, I followed her down the hall to her room. She motioned for me to sit in the chair, while she walked to the foot of the bed and sat on its edge. Her silence unnerved me. I was sure she could hear every thump of my heart. I tried to smile but couldn't.

"Helen," she said, "I'm really sorry about how I spoke to you the other day. I guess I let my feelings build up for too long. I should have said something sooner. The truth is, I am jealous of you and the time you have to study. I never had that. I know it's wrong for me to begrudge you something I didn't have. Will you forgive me?" I was totally unprepared for her confession of jealousy of me, something I'd never suspected. Nor had I ever encountered such honest self-revelation.

"Of course, Anna, of course I forgive you. Though our situations are very different, I can understand why you would feel this way."

She went on to tell me about her younger days, and the difficult times that she had survived. We did not become friends, but we did connect at a deep level, thanks to her courageous willingness to reach out to me, to reveal an undesirable truth about herself, and to ask my forgiveness. I learned an invaluable lesson that day—to speak my truth, even when it's messy, as a way of respecting and embracing myself, as well as the other.

In June of 1983, I left Memphis and headed back to St. Louis with a heavy heart, diploma in hand and a new assignment as the first Mission Coordinator for the SSM Health Care System. I would miss my Memphis friends, but I felt stronger and more self-confident than when I left St. Louis two years earlier. I believed I could create and develop this corporate-level position, though I continued to have some real doubts about my personal and professional capabilities.

My two-year sojourn away from home allowed me to expand my world view, and through my experiences to also become more aware of my own inner world. I liked much of what I discovered within myself, but so much more remained closed off and disconnected. There was still a part of me that felt ashamed, guilty, and unworthy, that child-self who had run away and hidden when my dad beat my mom. No one, not even me, could like and accept her. I didn't want to look at that part of me and feel the shame and guilt. Because I chose to ignore such a significant part of my inner world, I continued to feel insecure and handicapped in my responses to many situations. Despite these limitations, my next two years as Mission Coordinator went well professionally.

Personally, I was about to begin a different kind of journey, a deeper spiritual journey that would bring me face to face with the part of me that I hated and had abandoned. In fact, this journey would lead to my hospitalization and subsequent resignation of my two-year stint as Mission Coordinator at the end of 1985.

The years that led up to the painful events of the fall of 1985 also prepared me for a dramatic turn in my life that would end with my leaving the Community. Those years had been marked by discovery, depression, dissolution, and darkness. Through all the peaks and valleys of that long journey, I had gradually emerged from my denial and admitted the painful family secret that I had buried deeply with my own brokenness. Along the way, so many women and men crossed my path and sometimes stayed for a while. They offered their presence, their care and support, their teaching, their struggle, and often their friendship. I believe these relationships, these connections, softened me with compassion and prepared me to face the inner self that I had abandoned. Prior to this softening, I had resisted life, especially those situations that did not meet my expectations, which were based on my distorted perceptions of reality. I didn't know how to trust and knew little of acceptance, forgiveness, or the compassionate embrace. But now, I looked out at the world with a little less fear and looked inside myself with a desire to love the unacceptable part of myself that I so harshly judged.

My personal transformation had a mental, emotional, and spiritual impact. Like most survivors of a chaotic, abusive family environment, I've always craved order. Yet, this whole process of self-transcendence that can result in transformation is messy and defies description. Dante comes close in Canto I of his Divine Comedy:

> At the mid-point of the path through life, I found
> Myself lost in a wood so dark, the way
> Ahead was blotted out. The keening sound
> I still make shows how hard it is to say
> How harsh and bitter that place felt to me—
> Merely to think of it renews the fear—
> So bad that death by only a degree
> Could possibly be worse.

Yes! I have been there, lost and stalked by fear. Perhaps you also know the experience. As a small child, I was terrified and helpless. My trek through life seemed impossible at times, and yet I was resilient. Rather than let my heart harden in bitterness, I felt my pain, and in time I accepted the truth of who I am—broken, wounded, but lovable and healable.

The most important part of my story I long to share with you is this: What really matters is not that Mom abandoned me emotionally, nor the fact that I learned to abandon myself and did so for many years. What is most important is the power of the relationships that helped me accept and embrace my broken self.

This embrace was possible because of the love and acceptance I received through my connection with others, my relationships. We cannot do this alone. It is our inner journey, but we must have the feedback and support of other people.

This inner journey is often precipitated by a crisis or a painful experience that requires us to look within where we risk meeting up with that unloved part we believe ourselves to be, the part we have abandoned. But deep within is also where we encounter our best and highest self, whose capacity to love and forgive and to seek truth and beauty wants to be embraced and needs to be expressed. At this deep level, we not only experience our connection with one another but also integrate the lessons of our journey, replace our distorted beliefs, and make changes that reveal the truth of who we really are.

I now see myself through the eyes of compassionate forgiveness, which allows me to live a new life, free from the conditioned beliefs and behaviors that plagued my young adult years. My journey to freedom has been arduous. The journey *is* the process that transformed me from a terrified child into a loving adult. I want that for you, too. I encourage you to take heart and know that you are not alone.

Chapter Twenty

LESSONS FROM THE HEART

"I don't want to get rid of that sadness; it's part of who I am today. I feel like it's a fertile soil at the bottom of my heart where everything grows—creativity, compassion, love and even joy."
—Isabel Allende

It was the trees that saved me. Whenever I could, I ran to the woods where I felt their benevolent welcome to escape my father's violence. I wandered among those tall sentinels the way a baby elephant weaves in and out of the legs of the giant adults, safe and protected. There I felt the connection of the trees and sky and earth and all its creatures. The water, plants, and rocks were my companions, quietly sustaining me in the midst of those terrifying years. The energy of nature's embrace kept calling me back and challenged me to find my way without fearing the bend in the path just up ahead. The silent comfort and interconnectedness of nature made me think that maybe God was really there. I could sit, lean against an old oak, and not say a word. It was a safe and sacred space.

Today, when I look at a tree—really look at it—I remember the pain and the comfort. I cannot separate the two. The trees became part of my life when pain cried out so silently that only the aged oaks could hear and understand. I went to them with my sadness, my fear, and a heart full of tears for which I had no words. A deep longing drew me to the woods where, through layers of seasons, the trees had learned to weather the storms and remain standing strong. They taught me the wisdom of stillness, of presence, and perseverance. They comforted me with their protective shade. Their accumulated seasons of endurance gave me hope for a new and better season for my own life.

A friend recently told me that the word for tree in Celtic Irish means "learning." The ancient Celts honored trees as spiritual beings of wisdom. The trees were among my first teachers. When I learn, I perceive things differently, I change my experience, and in the process, I am transformed. As a child, I learned through curiosity, observation, absorption, and repetition. Because I lost some of these skills in the transition to adulthood, I've struggled at times to keep an open mind, to explore, to listen, to let go of distorted and/or outdated beliefs. I credit my mother for my thirst to learn. One of the few stories I recall her telling was that she was not allowed go to high school because her father didn't want her to have to live in town where she would be exposed to corrupting influences. She always ended the story with the regret that she was denied the opportunity for more education. I think that's why she made so many sacrifices to be sure that my sisters and I went to high school.

Mom took good care of us in many ways, but in the presence of her husband's brutality, she was helpless to care for herself or us. She never acknowledged our dad's abuse, much less talked with us about it or told us what to do when it occurred. If we were in the room when he attacked her, she never told us to leave, never took any steps to protect us from the horror of what took place. I was caught in a dilemma: Should I stay and try to protect her or take my sisters away, so they could not see or hear his abuse? Because of Mom's gross disconnect from us, I learned that I could not count on her, even though I wanted to.

As a child and beyond, I was full of anger toward her because she didn't leave my father and take us away from the violence. However, as an adult, my perception of her changed, and I came to view her as a survivor, ready to learn and broaden her world. I appreciated her resilience and realized that in the midst of her painful struggles, she had passed that gift on to my sisters and me. When Mom died in 2002, I realized that her life of eighty-one years was not defined by her suffering but by her choice to emerge from victimhood and take charge of her life. I am in awe of the power of her legacy, those lessons from the heart she never spoke aloud but simply lived.

In the ten years after Mom's death, my life flowed smoothly despite a growing restlessness within me. I started to write this book, and the process brought me face-to-face with my child-self that I was forced to encounter after all these years. I attended a workshop titled True Selves Rising and was impressed by the presenter, a psychotherapist who specialized in inner child work. I sensed she had something that I needed. Two days later, I sat in her office, not sure I was ready to engage with the child within me. It was almost as if that child had brought me there and was pleading with me to pay attention to her. It's true. I had a long way to go in terms of fully embracing this child that I had so wantonly abandoned over and over again.

My first session laid the groundwork for the most difficult therapy I've ever experienced. Once I shared my story, the remainder of my therapy was accomplished through drawing, coloring, and visualizations. Everything in me resisted these forms of expression. Of course, it was quite effective because these were ways of accessing my subconscious where I had hidden what now demanded my attention.

On August 10th at 9:15 a.m., my therapist's soft, peaceful voice guided the adult me into that space where our old house stood. "Now visualize yourself, Helen, walking up to the house. What do you see?" I was amazed at how clearly I could see the house we had lived in during those terrifying grade school years.

The cow munched grass off to the side. Towels hung on the clothesline. I opened the door and stepped into the kitchen. The house seemed empty. I called to my child.

"Helen, are you here?" No response. I walked cautiously up the steps to our old room. There, by the little window where I use to sit in the moonlight, sat a little girl. It was me. She sat on the floor and faced the window with a book on her lap, long hair falling over her little shoulders. I stood at the top of the steps as I spoke. "Helen, it's me—your older self."

She turned and looked at me over her shoulder, then went back to her book. She seemed so sad, so shy. I wanted to pick her up and hug her to my heart, but I didn't want to scare her. While I felt remorse that I had abandoned her, it was too soon to say I'm sorry. I moved closer and stooped, looking into her eyes.

"Helen, I want to spend time with you. So I will be back, if that's okay." She lifted her face and looked into my eyes, then shook her head yes. "I have something for you." I spoke softly. "It's a coloring book."

"Thank you," was all she said. She took the book and paged through it.

"I'll be back," I assured her and left in tears.

My attention came back to my therapist's office, but I was barely aware of her presence. I sobbed through what seemed like endless tears. I felt sad and alone and abandoned, just like that little child. These were the feelings I had carried deep within my soul all the years of my life. Most important of all, I now knew that I had to stop abandoning myself—which is what had happened every time I ignored my needs, my preferences, my opinions, every time I made a choice that violated my truth, every time I failed to speak up when something in me sought expression.

After this session, I didn't know if I could do this work. I knew I needed to face that child again, but my feelings overwhelmed me. Fortunately, my therapist suggested a technique I had read about earlier that year, and it intrigued me.

"What if," she said, "that child who was so full of fear had been visited by her future self, the adult you are now?"

I thought about this. I, her future self, could have listened to her, comforted her, and shown her who she would become. I imagined how different life would have been for her. This technique, coupled with using my imagination, was one way I could relate to that child now, which would allow me to release the painful energy.

My next session held a wonderful surprise. Guided by my therapist, I once again approached the old house that harbored so many painful memories. To my delight, I saw little Helen's face peeking through the kitchen window. She was waiting for me! She waved with an eagerness I had not expected. The door flew open, and she ran down the steps and into my arms. I held her for awhile and felt her arms circle my neck. My heart leaped in my chest. She wiped my tears with her little hand, and I tasted hers as I kissed her cheeks. We laughed. I never wanted to let her go. She wanted to show me what she had colored.

"See what I've done!" she said as she held her book up to me. We sat on the bench, and I looked at every picture.

"These are beautiful, Helen. I really like the colors you've chosen," I said and hugged her again.

I asked her if she was alone, and she said, "No. Mom's here, but you can't see her."

In the days that followed, I often thought about this little girl, and I felt her aloneness. One evening, I sat on my porch to watch the moon rise. I had often done this with my grandmother when I was a little girl. For a moment, I closed my eyes and listened to the tree frogs. Suddenly, I was aware of a small presence. She climbed into the lawn chair next to me and sat silent. I smiled and opened my arms to her.

"Helen, would you like to sit on my lap?" With a smile, she shook her head yes as she came and stood next to me. I lifted her on to my lap. "How was school today?"

With great excitement she told me how she was learning to read and about what she did at recess. "We played hide and seek and guess what? They had a hard time finding me."

She asked me about the night sounds. I sang her a lullaby, and soon she laid her head on my chest and fell asleep. When I eventually opened my eyes, she was gone, but my connection with her was strong and real.

In a subsequent therapy session, I was asked to use crayons to draw my child-self. "Where have you placed her?" my therapist asked.

"She is in front of the old house, playing with her doll," I responded.

"Now, close your eyes, and see your mom there with her. Does anything shift within you when you see your mom?"

I was not prepared for this. I closed my eyes, full of feelings I could not identify. I could not speak. Then Mom turned to leave. I couldn't call to her.

The therapist encouraged me. "Ask her if she loves you."

I felt awkward, but with eyes still closed, I said, "Mom, do you love me?" She turned to face me.

"Of course I love you, Helen. You are very special to me." I watched her bend to pick little Helen up and hold her close. I started to cry hard. I had so longed to hear her say those words.

"Now, Helen," my therapist said, "see your adult self come around the corner and into the scene. You are the future self of this child. It's time for you to claim her." I wondered how to do that, how to claim this child as part of myself. My therapist's voice was gentle but firm. "Take the child from your mother."

At that moment, I became the child, not my adult self, and I clung fast to my mother. I felt wanted. I knew the bad stuff my dad did wasn't her fault. I didn't want to let go of Mom.

My therapist spoke softly to my child self. "Helen, it's time for you to align with your adult self."

As the adult, I reached over and took Helen from Mom's arms. I held her close for a long time and promised, "I will never leave you, Helen. I will never abandon you again. I promise."

That was a powerful, pivotal moment in my therapy, not just because I promised that I would never abandon her/myself again, but because, for the first time ever, I felt that my mother really wanted and loved me. Perhaps that love had always been inside her, but because she was so emotionally detached, she never said "I love you," and I never felt her love. Now I felt it, and it was real.

Although it was difficult for me to take the child from my mother, I needed to claim her and begin to give her a different experience. For too many years I had denied, negated, ignored, or minimized my own needs, wants, and desires. In doing so, I had continued the abandonment that my mother initiated.

I drove home, saturated with feelings I could not identify as either sadness or joy, so mixed were they.

The next day I stared out my window and reflected on this amazing experience, feeling whatever it was I felt. I thought about the messages I had received and believed as a child and how wrong they were. All my life I had made choices based on those distorted beliefs, choices that had drastically limited me, choices to believe the lies, and consequently, abandon myself. But when I tapped into my subconscious by using my imagination and visualization, I was able to re-interpret my life experience from a new perspective and give it different meaning. Now that I saw the truth, I cried again. I felt anger, sadness, shock, relief, joy, and hope—all rolled into one unnamable feeling. I mainly felt relief that I could finally drop the burden I had carried all those years.

Here was the truth: *I never was broken or bad.* I had always been whole and loveable, with unlimited possibilities. Once I realized this, I felt like my life had been given back to me. Yet, in order to receive this gift, I had to let go of the burden. I would have to change the patterns I'd developed as a result of those distorted beliefs—the very patterns that had helped me survive.

This is where my promise to my child-self became significant. Honoring that promise gave me the fuel I needed to make choices that would honor that child, to strengthen my relationship with myself, and to help me integrate my past and my current life. I had to convince that child that I would always take care of her. I had to do things differently.

I would soon be tested on this.

Shortly after I made that promise, a friend invited me out for the evening. I said "Sure, I'll meet you there."

I hung up the phone and immediately felt an inner nudge. *Helen, what are you doing? You're tired, you've had a full day, and you know you don't want to go out.* Then I remembered the promise and realized that, once again, I had ignored my own needs. I was abandoning myself again, breaking my promise to pay attention to and take care of myself.

I called my friend back. "Ellen, I'm sorry, but I really need to stay home tonight." I knew that, regardless of her response, I had to be true to myself and keep my promise. Gradually, I began to change the abandonment patterns that had plagued me for so long. This was a promise I could not afford to break.

My therapy ended after twelve sessions, partly because of time constraints and partly because of the cost, but mainly because I had received enough to work with for a while. It's been a challenge to remember that I am the future self of a small child, a child to whom I made a promise. That child also wants me to play with her after so many years of no play at all. Although I'm not so good at it, I desire with all my heart to be able to play and to develop my creativity, which could be a whole new resource for modifying my survival skills and creating new patterns for responding to life.

While it may be a difficult concept to grasp, I believe that just as I am the future self of that child, I also have a future self who already knows how I will navigate these next few years. I want to explore ways to relate with my future self, trusting that she is not only older but also wiser and playful. I believe she can make a difference in my life now if I use those tools of imagination and visualization to tap into her presence. Perhaps there are things she already knows that she could teach me. Could this be a resource we all have access to if we only learn how?

My mom also eventually grew into her future self. I watched her struggle to rise above the broken life she once had, a life that was never safe for either her or her children. Not until my late forties did I learn, through therapy, that most of my deep, violent anger was directed towards my mom, rather than my dad and his brutality. I blamed her for not taking us out of that terrifying situation. That was her great sin. When I began work with abused women in my fifties, I learned so much from them that helped me understand my own mother. I learned that there were numerous reasons why she, like so many other abused women, chose to stay with her abuser, such as:

- She didn't know where to go with three small children.
- She was physically and financially dependent on him.
- She believed that if she tried hard enough, she could change him.
- She risked more injury, even death if she tried to leave.
- She still loved him.

As I worked with women caught in violent relationships, I began to understand the effect the abuse had on them as they struggled to survive. I eventually stopped blaming my mom and began to forgive her.

It did not come easy. Forgiving her was a slow process that required me to first recognize the wounds I suffered as a child. Next I had to claim them, feel the pain, and in time, identify what lay below that pain: the sense of abandonment, the grief for all the loss, and the pervasive fear that dictated all my choices. Many of my therapy sessions involved the expression of deep grief as I struggled to accept what had happened to me and to my family. A wise spiritual guide helped me through part of the process.

"Acceptance doesn't mean that what happened to you was acceptable," she said. "It simply means that you accept what is. It happened. You can't deny it."

The truth was that I had denied it for years. She continued. "When you accept the truth of what happened, you will hopefully release any resentment or anger that lingers in your heart."

"I don't know how to do that," I said.

She thought for a while and then suggested, "Maybe, if you look at your parents through different eyes, you will see their vulnerability. With compassion, you might change how you interpret what happened. You might even write a new narrative where you empower yourself with what you've learned through this experience."

This made sense to me. "So forgiveness is about my choice to change my perspective and create my own experience of healing?"

"That's a big part of it," she said. "But remember, it's a process. Let it evolve."

In time, I saw Mom in a different light. My heart softened, and I gradually forgave her. Even as I write this, it occurs to me that lessons from Mom's heart emerged as I observed her over the years. I absorbed those unspoken lessons that she taught through the choices she made, and they have strongly influenced who I am today. The following is the legacy she passed to me, a legacy of strength and resilience.

I can do this. As a small child, I watched Mom cook, clean, and then go find and milk the cow after a long a day of working at her factory job. She never complained, even though at the end of the day, she still had to deal with her physically and emotionally abusive husband. Many times I've said to myself, "I can do this," as I've faced challenges much smaller than hers. Her life exemplified this powerful statement.

I am not a victim. My father's abusive control extended to all aspects of Mom's life. When my sisters and I were small, we spent many hours sitting in the car with her outside a tavern until he was ready to leave. Whether it was hot or cold, we waited. If he was in a bad mood, he would decide not to take Mom to get groceries after all. In her mid-forties she decided to do something about this.

I got a call from Mom one day. She was excited. "Helen, I got my driver's license today."

"You what? Mom, how did you learn to drive?" I could sense her smile at the other end of the line.

"Well, I drove the car up to the store parking lot and practiced. Remember, I drove a tractor on the farm before I met your dad."

"So how is he dealing with this?" I asked.

"What could he say? I'm tired of waiting for him to take me to get groceries." She was beginning to find her way beyond his total control.

I can always start over. Because of the choices my father made, we moved approximately fifteen times during my childhood. Each time, Mom was the one who figured out how to get what we needed to live in our new location. She found the schools. She found work and a way to get there. When our dad died, she did what she had to do to adjust to widowhood. She started over once again, only this time she did what she wanted to do. And she thrived! I've had many endings and new beginnings in my life, and have faced them with a sense of confidence that came from watching her.

I'm worth it. It took a while for Mom to believe that she was worthy and deserving. It was only after my father's death that she began to live this. Once, when I asked her what her biggest learning was after his death, she replied, "becoming my own person."

I remember a story my sisters told me about going with her to find and purchase a new home. Mom planned to live near my sister Carol Ann, who had always been close to Mom and was very committed to watching out for her. When she bought her new place, Mom also decided to buy all new furniture.

"Everything I have is old or was used before I got it. I think it's time I got something new," she said. "I'm worth it." Despite all the abuse, she had learned a significant lesson that my sisters and I still grapple with today.

Plant and enjoy the fruits of your labors. Mom always had a vegetable garden, no matter the circumstances, and she set aside one corner of the garden for her flowers—cosmos, zinnias, and rose moss. She gave each of us a tiny plot to plant our own rose moss. I still enjoy waiting for the delicate pink, orange, and yellow blossoms to show up each spring in my garden. Mom grew up tending gardens, from which her family gathered food to cook and store for the winter. As a child, I noticed that when she worked with her plants, she seemed more relaxed. She smiled. She coaxed the most wonderful vegetables and flowers from the earth.

I sometimes feel her presence as I plant, nurture, and gather herbs from the pots on my porch. Though it may not seem like a momentous activity, when I move into that plant space, my connection with Mom and with nature is reaffirmed, and I am more nurtured than the plants. This has become one of my most treasured resources.

I know that my feelings toward my mom have softened because the way I feel about myself has changed. I hardly recognize the person I once was. This transformation is nothing short of a miracle, a miracle rooted in the relationships that have challenged and enriched my journey.

In my younger years, I hid from everyone, including myself. I was gripped with fear that I would be discovered, and I lived in a self-imposed form of solitary confinement, safe from life except for what went on inside of me. I stood on the outside and looked in at a place I thought I could never be. It felt like a giant circle was drawn around everyone else, and I was always on the outside, unable to cross over the line. I longed to be with the others, even though I was determined to remain apart. Being disconnected from everyone and everything was my greatest misery.

But I changed. It's difficult to pinpoint what contributed most to my evolution. Was it my struggle to survive, or my mother's legacy, or the courage I mustered to face what I thought was a hostile world? Or was it the people in my life who helped me see the world in a new light?

So much of life is about how we choose, enter, nurture, negotiate—or eventually leave—our relationships. Some of my relationships were healthy while others were not. Now in my seventieth decade, I know that both the healthy and unhealthy had the potential to enrich me. Both played a role in my life and contributed something to my growth as a person, one way or another, through love or fear, joy or pain.

In the maze of our adult relationships, it's easy to forget that every child we encounter needs someone to show them that they are valued and cared for. It may be only a fragile, brief connection, but that energy can be given and received through a smile, a touch, or a word. When you connect with a child's heart, I can tell you from my own experience that the connection can be powerful enough to change a life. When Sister Adelbert saw that I was hurting and put her arm around my shoulder that day in the school yard, she made me feel worthy during one of the darkest times of my life. Her concern brightened my darkness and taught me a powerful life lesson about what can happen when we reach out to someone with care.

One of the ways our inner darkness can be transformed is when we trust ourselves enough to be vulnerable and offer compassion to another person. The human spirit is resilient, and it can work its way through the darkness until something changes that ignites the desire to help ourselves and other sufferers.

Even before our own wounds have healed, compassion can emerge. This is what led me, at the age of seventeen, to join a religious community of hospital sisters to serve God by taking care of the sick. At thirty-nine, I became a social worker because I felt I could help others through psychotherapy. At fifty-nine, I decided to work specifically with abused women, a work for which I had been well prepared. And at sixty-six, I decided to write my story, in hopes that it would help women with similar backgrounds to see my transformation and feel empowered to write a new script for themselves.

Is this difficult journey worth the effort? I assure you that it is. As I was transformed from that fearful, terrified child, I learned some valuable lessons that guided me to eventually accept and embrace the self I had learned to reject. I share these lessons with you and hope they will enlighten you and encourage you to open yourself to heal.

Emotional abandonment is about separation, loss of self, deeply rooted fear, and inner insecurity. When we are emotionally abandoned, it robs us of a healthy sense of self, and we feel bad about ourselves. We cannot see our own goodness, and so we continue the abandonment process. We continue to believe the distorted messages that we are bad, not worthy, not good enough, et cetera, and we treat ourselves accordingly.

We can stop the process that diminishes our value and sense of well-being by accepting the responsibility to change what we believe about ourselves. One way to do this is to reconnect with the child that we learned to abandon, and with help, identify ways to embrace that child through acceptance and forgiveness.

Forgiveness does not come easy because we must start by forgiving ourselves. It takes time to realize that, along with the hurt that others inflicted, we also blame ourselves for so much. As children, we accepted responsibility for things we could not control and have carried that guilt into adulthood. When we share our story with someone who listens with compassion, we can express our guilt, the anger that covers over the hurt, and grieve our losses. When we acknowledge our pain and take these steps to heal, we clear the way back to that deep place within us where we meet our true, resilient self. We are freed to eventually forgive those who have caused us pain.

Resilience is the capacity to respond effectively to adversity. When we reconnect with our true, authentic self, we discover that we are resilient. The false messages that said we were bad and unworthy were communicated before we were developmentally mature enough to dismiss them, so we believed them. We abandoned our true self and lived out those distorted beliefs. When we choose to believe the truth of our essential goodness and beauty, we find the strength and resourcefulness to create a new direction for our life. We make different choices and enjoy self-empowerment, perhaps for the first time. We also discover outside resources that can help us stretch our capacity to cope with adversity, as well as teach us to enjoy our life journey.

Strategies for survival that we developed in order to live in an abusive home were rooted in fear-based thoughts and behavior patterns. We were skilled at navigating the constant threats. Those same skills fostered strengths that we can now reshape into new skills, in order to live as a whole and healed person. When we identify how these negative patterns of thought and behavior interfere with our life, our inner resilience can help us reframe those negative patterns. We learn to accept, rather than judge, both ourselves and others.

Relationships can be a great source of joy; they can also cause us deep pain. We are created to be in relationships—with ourselves, with others, with the environment, and with God.

Without these relationships, we will continue to feel isolated and abandoned. When human relationships fail us, as they sometimes do, Nature welcomes us with her unconditional presence, energy, and shelter. In the stillness of the trees and forest floor, I have felt the loving presence of the One who created me for goodness and for beauty. Tuned into my own goodness, I have more to bring to my relationships. In the end, our relationships are our greatest treasure.

Wherever you are in your healing journey, take heart. You may feel stuck at times, but you don't need to remain there, even if the path is steep and rocky. I stumbled many times in my search for wholeness. It has taken a while for me to feel safe enough to share my story with you, but in the process, I now know that I am my own safe and sacred space. I needed to give up judgments about myself and embrace all that has gone into the making of who I am. I invite you to do likewise.

> You will discover that you are worthy and more than good enough.
>
> You can create a new direction in your life, rooted in your own resilience.
>
> You no longer need to be defined by your childhood pain.
>
> You can embrace your true self and become whole again.
>
> You can claim your own goodness and beauty.
>
> **You will become your own safe and sacred place.**

I Count

I am a person…I have a right to:
~see things from my own perspective
~think differently than others
~do things differently than someone else
~speak in my own voice

My opinion counts…
My wishes and preferences count…
My choices deserve to be respected

It's okay if I disagree with you
It's okay if you disagree with me

My differences reflect
~my individuality,
~my history
~my experiences
They are neither good nor bad
They are what they are

I am, in fact a unique expression of
The One who
Breathed me into Life
Whose life I breathe
I am cherished by this One
Who is Divine Love
I am Divine Love
I am

EPILOGUE

"And the day came when the risk to remain tight in a bud was more painful than the risk it took to blossom."

—Anaïs Nin

It Felt Love

How
Did the rose
Ever open its heart

And give to this world
All its
Beauty?

It felt the encouragement of light
Against its
Being,

Otherwise,
We all remain

Too

Frightened.

Hafiz

EVERY ENDING HAS
A NEW BEGINNING

The trauma of growing up with family violence has shadowed every phase of my life—as a single person, as a member of a religious community, as a married woman, and now as a widow. Along the way, through the mystery of maturing and with the support of others, I have begun to embrace both the painful and the joyful experiences as valuable parts of who I am.

Through it all, I have broken out of the contracted state in which I lived my earlier years when I was full of fear and did not believe in myself. But just as my journey continues, so does the periodic emergence of those old patterns—thoughts that limit me, feelings that escape me, behaviors that are tinged with insecurity. I can never forget from whence I have come.

The good news is that I not only survived the violence of my childhood, but I am also rising above the consequences of that darkness—one day at a time. I greet each new day, first with gratitude, and then with the awareness that no matter what happens this day, the skills I've honed along the way and the support of loved ones will get me through.

My heart still breaks when I hear of families victimized by the crime of domestic violence. I smile when I see a father walk down the sidewalk holding his child's hand. I cringe when I hear someone belittle another person. I feel hope when I remember that Mom gave my niece money to help her with her divorce so that she could get out of an abusive relationship. And I cry when I hear of another woman killed by her abusive partner.

I began this book as a true labor of love, out of the desire to help others heal. In the end, it has been a significant part of my own healing, a process that will continue beyond the completion of these pages.

We all share the human experience, characterized by wounds of some form. My hope for you, my reader, is that you have garnered something from my story that will move you to choose whatever it is that guides you to return to your true, sacred self with love and acceptance.

I leave you with a poem found among my mother's writings. The ninth line indicates that she wrote it before I left my religious community. Though Mom only had an eighth grade education, the poems, songs, and children's stories she wrote in her later years reflect a rich inner life that we never knew. I cherish the line in her poem where she says:

"And as I tell the world this story…And as I write this song this way…." She finally found her voice!

And I, too, have found mine.

You Were On My Mind Today

You were on my mind all day today and
I can't understand the reason why.
Unless it's because you are that way, more precious as the years go by
That's why
I'm singing this song to you; it will help me through the day
Because you will always be you
And you will always be that way
So many have felt your tenderness in so many things you do
So many would have lost their faith
If it had not been for you
You seem to leave a Presence on every one's path you cross
And the ones who have never met you yet
Will never know what they have lost
Many lives have changed somehow; everyone you touch
Now you know the reason you are loved so much.
And as I tell the world this story
And as I write this song this way
I now understand why
You are on my mind today.

by Sarah Elizabeth Coleman

My Mother

Sarah Elizabeth Coleman
On her 78th birthday

1920–2002

PART V

CREATING A NEW LIFE NARRATIVE

"Abandonment is a complex human issue, its wound deeply entrenched in fear and insecurity. Without recovery, abandonment can linger beneath the surface, undermining self esteem and sabotaging future relationships. The tools of healing help to reverse this injury. We build a new sense of self, increase our capacity for love, and find greater life and relationships than before."

—Susan Anderson
Black Swan: The Twelve Lessons of Abandonment Recovery

To create a new life narrative, we begin by acknowledging the old narrative—what happened, the pain, what we did to survive. Once we can accept all of this and embrace the self we abandoned, we allow the old experience to be integrated into who we are becoming, and we are freed to choose new, healthy ways of thinking, perceiving, and responding to life. We are empowered to create a new life experience.

Each item in this section is offered as a potential aid to help you grow in your own self-empowerment, a means to create a new way to perceive yourself, your life, and your relational environment. They are:

1. **Discussion Guide** – An opportunity to create a conversation around a topic that is usually difficult to talk about.

2. **Recommended Books** – Sources significant to my journey.

3. **Additional Reading** – An opportunity to expand your awareness and understanding of family violence, emotional abandonment, and healing.

4. **Other Resources** – Contact information for your reference.

5. **Appendices (4)** – Handouts that I have used with workshop participants. Each contains information for your study and reflection.

Disclaimer

The information provided here and throughout my book is intended to educate, motivate, and offer hope. Nothing herein is intended to diagnose or treat health issues. Neither is it a substitute for personal consultation with a qualified health or mental health professional. I cannot offer a promise or guarantee of specific results and therefore disclaim any liability incurred directly or indirectly resulting from the reader's choice to apply suggestions included in this material.

BOOK DISCUSSION GUIDE

The following questions are intended to guide readers in a meaningful discussion to enhance their experience of the book, to give them an opportunity to have a conversation about a topic that is usually difficult to address. The questions may also be used for personal reflection, which may provide new insights into the reader's experience.

1. The central issue in domestic/family violence is the abuser's need to control his or her partner. Sometimes the control is exercised overtly, as in cases of verbal and physical abuse. Sometimes it is not so obvious, as in cases of psychological and emotional abuse.

   How did Helen's father control the members of his family?

2. Helen wanted her mom to leave her husband and take her and her sisters away from the danger. The common belief, even today, is that a woman caught in this situation could leave if she really wanted to.

   What do you think?
   What do you understand about her alternatives?

3. In addition to feeling overly responsible, Helen took on the mothering role with her youngest sister and the role of protector with both her sisters.

   What impact did this have on Helen's life? On her family's life?

4. The early years of Helen's story took place in the 1940s and 1950s, when there was no support system for an abused woman and her family—particularly in a rural area.

   How did the lack of such resources affect Helen's mother? The entire family?

   What resources are available today?

5. What comes to mind when you hear the term *domestic or family violence?*

   Did you know that domestic violence is a crime?

   What is the core issue of this crime?

6. Do you know anyone who has or is experiencing family violence?

   How does knowing this affect you?

   What are your concerns?

7. Helen's mom experienced extreme abuse throughout her married life, yet she maintained the family, cared for three daughters, and worked outside her home.

   What qualities helped her do this and survive?

   What were her greatest challenges?

   What did she give up in the process?

8. Helen's experience of emotional abandonment was not only invisible to others, but it was unknown to herself until years later.

   What messages did she get from her mother that modeled self-abandonment?

   When did Helen begin to abandon herself?

   How did this play out in her adult life?

9. We seldom think about how children experience aloneness and what they do to cope with it.

    Were there times during your childhood when you felt alone, isolated, or abandoned?

    How did you respond to this experience? Who did you talk with about it?

10. Review the Patterns described in Chapter Sixteen. As indicated, these can be a result of a variety of dysfunctional situations experienced when growing up.

    Are there any patterns that feel familiar to you?

    How do they affect your life?

    What are some things that you can do to change the patterns?

11. In her July 11, 1985 journal entry (Chapter Seventeen), Helen expressed that she felt abandoned by God.

    Can you relate to this experience?

    What helped you get through it?

12. What was the first major decision Helen made?

    How do you feel about the choice she made?

13. Does any particular story from Part II speak to you?

    How do you relate with it?

14. Discuss Helen's relationship with Nature.

    How did the trees save her?

    How do you relate with Nature?

15. There are three turning points in Helen's story, when a flash of awareness brought her to a new level of consciousness.

    a. Chapter Seventeen: "My dad beat my mom."

    b. Chapter Seventeen: "I realized I was not bad, and I wasn't broken."

    c. Chapter Nineteen: "I will never leave you, Helen. I will never abandon you again. I promise."

    Discuss how each of these pivotal moments changed the direction of her journey.

    Have you ever experienced such a moment? What difference did it make in your life?

Don't let your past define you,
but let your past be a part of
who you are becoming.

—My Big Fat Greek Wedding

RECOMMENDED BOOKS

The information, strength, and guidance that I found through the following four books helped me navigate the unfamiliar journey that led me to wholeness and healing. These are only a few of the resources I drew from.

Black Swan: The Twelve Lessons of Abandonment Recovery by Susan Anderson

Susan Anderson presents *Black Swan* as an allegory that is designed to help adults internalize a message of healing. The Black Swan is a symbol for healing, a spirit guide for overcoming the woundedness of abandonment. "The lessons take us through the recovery process step by step—from discovering our center, to developing a new sense of self, and finally to making a new connection."

Enhancing Resilience In Survivors of Family Violence by Dr. Kim Anderson

Dr. Kim Anderson's book is based on the research program in which I participated. While it focuses more on educating, it contains amazing stories of women survivors. She highlights these key topics:

- Dynamics and consequences of family oppression and violence
- The power of recovery and posttraumatic growth
- Assessments that capture client strengths, resilience and acts of resistance

- Spirituality: making meaning of one's trauma and purpose in life.

Anderson underscores the resourcefulness of her clients and illuminates the many ways people prevail during and in the aftermath of family violence.

Bouncing Back: Rewiring Your Brain For Maximum Resilience and Well-Being by Linda Graham, MFT

Linda Graham, MFT, has written effectively about resilience as the ability to face and handle life's challenges, whether everyday disappointments or extraordinary disasters. She also provides us with a practical guide that integrates mind, body, and spirit through the use of practice guides. Her book is groundbreaking in that it brings together ancient wisdom, relational psychology, and modern neuroscience.

The Spontaneous Healing of Belief: Shattering the Paradigm of False Limits by Gregg Braden

Gregg Braden is internationally renowned as a pioneer in bridging science and spirituality. He helps us understand the role of beliefs in our life, how a change in our perceptions—a shift in our beliefs—holds a timeless secret to healing, peace, and even reality. He maintains that the key to healing is to understand what belief is and how it works in our life. Much of our struggle to move beyond our wounds is due to our limited beliefs. The author invites us to move beyond these false limits.

ADDITIONAL READING

When Dad Hurts Mom: Helping Your Children Heal the Wounds of Witnessing Abuse by Lundy Bancroft, 2004

Healing Your Emotional Self: A Powerful Program to Help You Raise Your Self-Esteem, Quiet Your Inner Critic, and Overcome Your Shame by Beverly Engel, 2007

Changing Course: Healing from Loss, Abandonment, and Fear by Claudia Black, Ph.D., 1999

The Emotionally Abused Woman: Overcoming Destructive Patterns and Reclaiming Yourself by Beverly Engel, M.F.C.C., 1990

Outgrowing the Pain: A Book for and About Adults Abused As Children by Eliana Gil, Ph.D., 1983

Shame & Guilt: Masters of Disguise by Jane Middelton-Moz, 1990

Healing the Shame That Binds You by John Bradshaw, 1933

Crawling Out: One Woman's Journey to an Empowered Life after Breaking a Cycle of Abuse No One Should Have to Endure by Casey Morley, 2014

The Power of Resilience by Robert Brooks, Ph.D., Sam Goldstein, Ph.D., 2001

True Self-Love: Heal the Old Wounds and the Self-Love Will Come On Its Own by Alexander Janzer, 2013

Healing Is Remembering Who You Are: A Guide for Healing Your Mind, Your Emotions, and Your Life by Marilyn Gordon, 2013

Lost In The Shuffle: The Co-Dependent Reality by Robert Subby, 1987

Raising Resilient Children by Robert Brooks, Ph.D., Sam Goldstein, Ph.D., 2001

The Secret of the Shadow: The Power of Owning Your Whole Story by Debbie Ford, 2002

Healing the Child Within: Discovery and Recovery for Adult Children of Dysfunctional Families by Charles L. Whitfield, M.D., 1987)

When Violence Begins At Home: A Comprehensive Guide to Understanding and Ending Domestic Violence by K.J. Wilson, 2005

Getting Free: You Can End Abuse and Take Back Your Life by Ginny NiCarthy, 2004

The Courage To Heal: A Guide for Women Survivors of Child Sexual Abuse by Ellen Bass & Laura Davis, 1994

Helping Her Get Free: A Guide for Families and Friends of Abused Women by Susan Brewster, 2006

Trust After Trauma by Aphrodite Matsakis, 1998

The Language of Letting Go: Daily Meditations for Codependents by Melody Beattie, 1990

Radical Acceptance: Embracing Your Life with the Heart of a Buddha by Tara Brach, Ph.D., 2003

My love for trees prompts me to include the names of some of the books that I have come to appreciate. These volumes have inspired and nurtured my connection with our beloved trees that contribute so much to our well-being and that of our planet. Enjoy!

The Tree That Survived the Winter by Mary Fahey, 1989

The Attentive Heart: Conversations with Trees by Stephanie Kaza, 1993

The Giving Tree by Shel Silverstein, 1999

The Man Who Planted Trees by Jean Giono, 1985

A Tree Grows in Brooklyn by Betty Smith, 1943

OTHER RESOURCES

Important Contacts

National Domestic Violence Hotline
800-799-7233

National Center for Victims of Crime Hotline
800-273-8255

National Resource Center on Domestic Violence
www.nrcdv.org

National Coalition Against Domestic Violence
www.ncadv.org

National Children's Alliance
www.nationalchildrensalliance.org

National Child Traumatic Stress Network
www.nctsn.org

National Alliance on Mental Illness
www.nami.org

Futures Without Violence
www.futureswithoutviolence.org

Love Is Respect Program for Teens & Parents
www.loveisrespect.org

Missouri Coalition Against Domestic and Sexual Violence
www.mocadsv.org

Woman's Place (St. Louis, MO)
www.womansplacestl.org

APPENDIX I

WHY SHE STAYS

There are many reasons why it's difficult for women to leave an abusive relationship. Here are some of the primary reasons.

Economic/Financial

- She is unable to support herself and her children.
- There is a lack of affordable housing.
- She is unable to pay medical expenses, rent, etc.
- There is a lack of transportation/childcare/other resources.
- It is possible that she would lose her own job.

Emotions/Beliefs

- She loves her partner (abuse often starts after relationship has been established).
- She hopes that he will change (abuser often promises he will do better).
- She feels guilty; she believes she has failed as a partner, mother, or person and assumes blame for the abuse.
- She is emotionally dependent on her abuser.
- She believes she is responsible for keeping the family together and wants the children to have a father.
- She believes she must try everything she can to make it work.
- She has strict religious beliefs regarding marriage.
- She has disabling symptoms of Post-Traumatic Stress Disorder (PTSD) caused by the violence.

- She feels hopeless.

- She experiences confusion/depression/anxiety/shame.

- She has low self-esteem.

Fear

- There's a good chance he will kill her if she leaves.

- She remembers the trauma when she tried to leave before.

- He threatens the safety of her children or other family members.

- She has never been alone.

- She may lose the support of family and friends.

- He will be violent when she tries to leave.

- She might lose her children.

Other

- She is socially isolated; isolation is often created by the abuser.

- She doesn't want anyone to know she's being abused.

- She has no place to go.

- She regards the abuse as normal because she grew up with family violence.

- She has traditional values.

- There are issues with child custody.

APPENDIX II
THE EFFECT OF FAMILY VIOLENCE ON US AS CHILDREN

There are multiple factors that influence how children who witness and grow up with family violence are impacted, such as:

- The age/stage of development/gender of the child.
- The level of violence/degree of exposure/length of time of the abuse.
- The relationship to the non-abusive parent.
- The presence of at least one significant, caring person in the child's life.

These children are traumatized on multiple levels:

Physical

Behaviors may include bedwetting, problems eating or sleeping, stress-related illness, and physical injury.

Emotional

Feelings of guilt, fear (including the fear of abandonment), sadness, anxiety, loneliness, depression, and anger (which covers over a multitude of painful feelings), limited ability to identify feelings; emotional abandonment by mother; learned self-abandonment; and problems creating healthy relationships.

Psychological

Problems may include persistent anxiety, hyper-vigilance, PTSD, boundary issues, and the inability to trust. They may be either aggressive or timid, and may have a distorted sense of self or a distorted sense of normalcy.

Other effects of family violence on children:

- They may experience multiple losses, including the relationship with the abusing person, the loss of childhood, the loss of safety, and loss of carefree play.

- They have a sense of responsibility for what is happening but have no voice to address it.

- Their choices are based on fear, shame, silence, and secrecy—rooted in distorted beliefs.

- They have distorted beliefs about self, others, situations, etc. (e.g. anger causes violence).

- They develop survival strategies that create problems in adult life, such as people-pleasing, the need to control, perfectionism, etc.

The key to addressing these effects:

If we can identify the strengths that helped us resist and survive the trauma of family violence, we can redefine our experience, rather than allow it to define us, and integrate it into our ongoing experience by rewriting our life script from a position of strength.

APPENDIX III
STRATEGIES FOR SURVIVAL: INNER PATTERNS

Inner Patterns are:

- The conditioned ways of thinking, feeling, and behaving that habitually guide our response to life.

- A collection of thoughts, feelings, and behaviors that are based on certain assumptions about the self, the world, and how we are to relate to each.

- These patterns are familiar and comfortable but also confining. They are sometimes rooted in distorted thinking. Because of our investment from an early age, it requires conscious awareness to change.

What these Patterns look like:

1. **A poor sense of self.** Perceive self as inferior to others, have little or nothing to offer, undeserving, unworthy, inadequate, define self by what we think others think of us, don't want anyone to know how lacking we are.

2. **Invisibility.** Choose not to be seen or heard, silent, don't speak up/express self, pretend all is well, withhold information to avoid certain reactions, avoid the limelight, fear of being "found out."

3. **People-pleasing.** Defer to others needs/preferences while minimizing and/or denying our own, overly compliant, always accommodating the other, fear rejection.

4. **Perfectionism.** See self as not able to do something well enough, need to re-do it in an effort to do it perfectly,

question our abilities, fail to start a project out of fear of not doing it well enough, withhold expressing self for fear of "not doing it right."

5. **Need for order.** Because of our discomfort with unpredictability, chaos, conflict, etc. we seek relief and comfort. Creating and maintaining order in our external environment helps us meet this need.

6. **Need to control.** Extending beyond the need to manage our external environment, there is a need to manipulate people, situations, and outcomes. The locus of control is "out there."

7. **Over-responsibility.** Assuming responsibility for another person or a situation, we also feel responsible for the outcome. This can give us the illusion of being "worthwhile." It also provides an escape from taking responsibility for our own issues.

8. **Minimize our own needs, wants, feelings, etc.** Rooted in a poor sense of self, it is difficult to recognize our own needs, wants, etc., and when we do, we ignore them. So focused on the other, we may not even notice our own underlying feelings and needs.

9. **Boundary confusion.** Not feeling valued, boundaries (physical and emotional) that help identify who we are, are not developed. It is impossible to know where we end and the other begins. It is difficult to set limits; to say no, etc.

10. **Hyper-vigilance.** Always on the alert, we watch and listen for clues as to what might happen next. This requires us to tune into the other's mood, feelings, etc. as a way of readiness to protect ourselves and/or our loved ones, often anticipating the worst.

11. **Avoidance of conflict.** We make choices to avoid a person or situation that would involve some form of conflict that already exists or might be created. This involves modifying our communications, behavior, etc. to avoid something we cannot tolerate.

12. Take life and self too serious. We grew up so fast, there was little time to be carefree as a child. Living with daily threats, we closed off our painful feelings, but we also closed off the potential for feelings of joy. As adults, we are limited in our use of imagination, play, sense of humor, a positive perspective, etc.

Conclusion

In each of these patterns, we can see the evidence of learned self-abandonment. Having experienced emotional abandonment as a child, we fear further rejection by others. We long to be approved of and accepted by the other and, to this end, we reject our own feelings, opinions, needs, preferences, etc. in order to accommodate the other and avoid further abandonment.

The challenge: To find and claim the self we have disowned. This will require that we transform our patterns of thinking, feeling, and behaving, beginning with a conscious choice to change our perception of ourselves, to reclaim the entirety of who we are, with both our weaknesses and our strengths.

The good news: We have been resourceful in developing these patterns/survival skills, and this is evidence that we also have strengths to be identified and claimed!

APPENDIX IV

CHANGES WE CHOOSE TO MAKE

To Change Is:

To make or become different, to modify or alter, revise, rework, adjust, shift, create a new version, exchange for something else, replace with something else.

The Process of Personal Change

The process of making a change begins with a shift in our consciousness—an awareness of something we want to be different. Einstein said, "We can't solve a problem at the same level of consciousness at which it was created." A shift in our awareness of something we are dissatisfied with can be our first clue that the process of personal change is underway.

Elements of Change

- Conscious awareness of the need to change
- Identification of what specifically needs to change
- Conscious choice to make the change, commitment to do something different
- Identification of strengths we have available to support the change
- Identification of specific steps to take to make the change
- Creation of an environment to support the change (internal/external)

Creation of an environment (internal/external) to support the change

- *Internal Environment.* Our perceptions, beliefs, thoughts, and the feelings they trigger, are internal activities about which we can make choices. These activate chemicals in our body that affect our immune system as well as influence our behavior. What changes do we need to make in our perceptions/beliefs/thoughts in order to support our effort to change?

- *External Environment.* We humans need other humans to support our efforts to change. Whether it is a good friend, a partner, spouse, minister, or therapist—talking about our efforts to change and processing our experience with someone we trust will strengthen our perseverance and help keep us honest with ourselves.

So here we go!

What we resist persists and keeps us stuck. Once we identify the pattern that keeps us stuck in our conditioned way of responding to life, we:

- Accept/claim the pattern that keeps us stuck
- Replace the thoughts that nurture the undesirable pattern
- Make purposeful choices to change our behavior

Questions to consider

- What motivates me to make the change? What are the barriers?

- What have I learned about change in terms of setting priorities?

- What have I already done to begin changing the identified pattern?

- What helps me sustain the effort to change once I start?
- How do I respond when I "slip" and fail to follow through? (e.g. self-talk)
- How will I know when I have accomplished my goal to make the change?
- How will I celebrate my accomplishment?

ABOUT THE AUTHOR

Helen Coleman Gennari, MSW, LCSW, left home at age sixteen to find work in the city to help pay bills accumulated by her abusive father. When she joined a religious order of nuns a year later, she did not realize that she brought with her the childhood turmoil and pain that she had successfully buried.

Twenty-five years later, the trauma of her violent childhood caught up with her and she was hospitalized, deeply depressed. Thus began her journey of discovery and healing which included eventually making the painful decision to leave her Congregation. Her inner work required her to face and embrace the self she had abandoned. In time, she married the man who would become her best friend, and was devastated when he died of cancer ten years later.

Through her work as a licensed clinical social worker, psychotherapist, and advocate for abused women, Helen has taught and counseled many women toward self-empowerment. She continues to offer compassionate guidance and hope for healing, especially to women who have grown up with family violence. She believes that we can be more than survivors—that we can return to our true selves, replace the patterns that kept us imprisoned, and thrive as whole, happy persons.

www.HeartOfAnAbandonedDaughter.com

IN GRATITUDE

Through the many seasons of my life, I have journeyed beyond the pain of those childhood days and deep into the experience of healing with the loving support of so many persons, all of whom I hope to remember. With a grateful heart, I acknowledge and thank the following persons.

My Family:

My parents, who have passed on, gave me life and countless opportunities to grow and evolve as a person. My sisters, Carol Ann and Janice Faye, who walked most of the way with me and gave me an outlet for my caring nature during those painful times of helplessness. For other family members who have encouraged my writing, I am grateful.

Our Trees:

At times, the trees were my family and my teachers: my grand-mother's elm tree that mothered me, the trees in the old orchard that held me when I had nowhere else to go, and the trees in our woods that welcomed me when I ran away from the house and my father's violence. My connection with the trees deepens as they continue to teach me about remaining still and present, faithful and forgiving, no matter what.

My Primary Teachers:

There have been so many! Members of my religious community, colleagues, and friends who taught me through their stable presence, life examples, and sometimes, wise direction. Outstanding among these is my first grade teacher, Rose Ann (Johnson) Richards whose friendship I continue to cherish. Our periodic visits are a time of remembering her first class of students, of which I was one. I credit her with my love for books and all things related.

Other Teachers:

I am especially grateful for *Arts For The Soul* and its artistic director, John Sant' Ambrogio. This is where I began to hone my writing skills through the guidance of writing experts like Jill Murphy-Long, Susan L. de Wardt, and Fred Hunter, whose skills and encouragement helped me start writing this book.

Friends, colleagues and other associates:

- Dale Goldmacher read chapters and provided constructive feedback.
- Nancy Straatmann helped with some of the research.
- Anne Stuckel connected me with publisher Robin Tidwell who liked my proposal and sent it on to my book coach, Nancy L. Erickson, The Book Professor.
- Meg Selig and Linda Senn, local authors who have shared their insights with me.
- Kate Schroeder my therapist, who challenged me to face my child self.
- Kim Anderson, Ph.D., who in her research with survivors of family violence, was the first person to listen to my story.

- Pat Moore of Coventry, England and Stephanie Mines, Ph.D., both of whom provided me with material during the research phase of my book proposal

- MCADSV (Missouri Coalition Against Domestic and Sexual Violence), whose library provided material during the research phase of my book proposal.

- Woman's Place, St. Louis, MO, the only drop-in center for abused women in the region where I was employed and now volunteer with a staff of compassionate women from whom I am always learning.

- Nancy L. Erickson, The Book Professor, without whom this book may have never come to be. Her amazing dedication, compassionate guidance, and enduring support helped me to believe that I really could create a book that would make a difference.

- Lundy Bancroft, who first encouraged me to write this book, read the manuscript, and kept his promise to write the Foreword. What he wrote told me that he had truly heard my voice.

- And last, but not least—JETLAUNCH. Chris and his team created a seamless process for getting this book to publication. Their package of services is truly amazing, topped only by their friendly, professional, and supportive customer service that makes me want to start writing my next book so that I can continue working with these great folks.

With all my heart, I thank each of you who have walked some part of my journey with me and, in so doing, contributed to the creation of this book.